LOW-CARB VEGETARIAN COOKING

Low-Carb Vegetarian Cooking

150 entrées to make low-carb
vegetarian cooking easy and fun

SUE SPITLER

with Linda R. Yoakam, R.D.

SURREY
BOOKS
Chicago

LOW-CARB VEGETARIAN COOKING is published by
Surrey Books, Inc., 230 E. Ohio St., Suite 120, Chicago, IL 60611.

First edition: 1 2 3 4 5

This book is manufactured in the United States of America

Library of Congress Cataloging-in-Publication Data:

Spitler, Sue.
    Low-carb vegetarian cooking: 150 entrées to make low-carb vegetarian cooking easy and fun /
Sue Spitler with Linda R. Yoakam.
    p. cm.
    Includes index.
    ISBN 1-57284-077-3
    1. Low-carbohydrate diet—Recipes. 2. Vegetarian cookery. I. Yoakam, Linda R. II. Title.
    RM237.73.S69 2005
    641.5'6383—dc22
                              2004025256

Editorial services: Sara A. Reddington
Art direction, book design, and production: Joan Sommers Design, Chicago
Nutritional analyses: Linda R. Yoakam, R.D., M.S.

For prices on quantity purchases or for free book catalog, contact Surrey Books at the
above address or at www.surreybooks.com

This title is distributed to the trade by Publishers Group West.

Acknowledgements

Many thanks to everyone who helped with the creation of *Low-Carb Vegetarian Cooking: 150 Entrées to Make Low-Carb Vegetarian Cooking Easy and Fun.*

Linda Yoakam, R.D.,M.S., for her nutritional guidance and computer analyses, Sara Reddington for her editing expertise, Leona Pitej for her editorial assistance, and Publisher Susan Schwartz for her ongoing support.

Contents

Introduction

Judging by magazines at checkout stands, cookbooks on bookstore shelves, and the buzz around workplace watercoolers, low-carbohydrate eating is widely popular. But low-carb diet plans may also be confusing because no standard for what constitutes "low-carb" exists and because no consensus has been reached on the value of one diet plan over another. Before you commit yourself body and soul to a low-carb regimen, take a few minutes to read the following information about healthful—and successful—low-carb eating. After all, no diet or eating plan will work, not even low carb, if you can't stay on it for lack of variety or if long-term health concerns arise.

Low-Carb Vegetarian Cooking: 150 Entrées to Make Low-Carb Vegetarian Cooking Easy and Fun was not written to be yet another "diet" book. It is written for people like you, who have already chosen to follow a vegetarian eating pattern and now want to incorporate this into a low-carb lifestyle. But be advised that your eating plan should be under the guidance of a physician or registered dietitian, and be sure to read this short introduction on nutrients and the role they play in maintaining health. With a fuller understanding of what nutrients are and how each impacts your body, you can use *Low-Carb Vegetarian Cooking* to enjoy delicious recipes that help you lower and control carbs, control or lose weight, manage blood sugars, and lower the risk of heart disease.

HOW A LOW-CARB DIET WORKS

Let's start with basic nutrition. There are many kinds of nutrients, of which carbohydrates, or "carbs" for short, is just one. Other nutrients include proteins, fats, vitamins, minerals, and water. For the purposes of this book, we are concerned only with the nutrients that contain calories. These are: carbohydrates, fats, and protein. Whether trying to lose or maintain weight, improve blood sugar control, or prevent heart disease, calories count first, no matter what form they are in: carbs, fats, or proteins. And depending on your health goals, the idea is to find the balance of calories and nutrients that works best for you. No one diet works for all people.

Carbohydrates are the body's primary and preferred source of energy. When you eat carbs, the body converts them into glucose, or blood sugar, which the body's cells use for fuel. For your body to function well, the fuel needs to enter the cells in a controlled manner. When the sugars/carbohydrates enter your body, a hormone called insulin unlocks the body's cells, acting as a control on how much glucose gets in at one time. Optimal body function strives to maintain blood sugar levels without dramatic highs and lows.

In some cases, when too many carbohydrates enter the body too quickly, control is lost and blood sugars can "spill" out into the bloodstream, raising blood sugar levels. People with diabetes or impaired insulin function, must carefully control the carbs they eat to avoid extreme blood sugar levels. High blood sugar can cause the cells to become resistant to insulin and both high blood sugar and insulin resistance can lead to a host of health problems, up to and including prediabetes, diabetes with all of its complications, and raised triglycerides (blood lipids or fats) that are implicated in heart disease.

Carbohydrates contain four calories per gram. They can come in a simple form called sugar, commonly found in foods such as candy, soda pop, cakes, pies, cookies, and ice cream. Carbohydrates can also come in more complex forms, sometimes called starches, like bread, grains, vegetables, and fruits. And finally, carbohydrates come in an indigestible form called fiber, or roughage. Fiber is found in foods such as whole grains, fruits, and vegetables and is important because it helps to slow and regulate sugar entering the bloodstream. Fiber also provides other health benefits: it helps reduce cholesterol, aids digestion, and prevents constipation and possibly colon cancer.

After carbohydrates, fats are the body's secondary choice for energy, and they are also the preferred form of calories for storing body fat. Fat has nine calories per gram, more than twice as many calories per gram as carbs. Fat calories, however, do not raise blood sugar. Fat in a meal actually helps control weight because it increases digestion time and makes you feel full. When you eat fats, some will be used for energy, but excess amounts will be stored as body fat.

The fat calories you eat, if chosen wisely, can help prevent heart disease. For example, saturated fats and cholesterol in the diet are associated with heart disease, while foods high in omega 3 fatty acids, such as walnuts or flaxseed, are associated with improved heart health. Some fats, such as hydrogenated fats found in margarine, shortenings, and many packaged foods, contain trans-fatty acids, a form of fat associated with many health problems, including heart disease.

Your body's least favorite source of energy is protein because it takes longer to be converted into glucose. Proteins, with four calories per gram, are essential for growth and maintenance of muscle mass, but watch out for the fat that lurks within proteins, not only for weight control but also for your heart's health. When you eat protein it enters the small intestine where it is broken down into molecules of amino acids. These are absorbed into the bloodstream and sent to the liver where they may be converted into glucose, or blood sugar. However, the process takes some time and is not a major contributor to high blood sugar. The human body prefers to use amino acids to build new protein.

Three keys to long-term weight control and good health can be clearly stated: balance the amounts of carbohydrate, protein, and fat that your body needs to function properly; eat healthful foods, such as carbs high in fiber and healthy fats; and burn excess calories by activity and exercise.

KEEPING CARBS LOW

How low is a low-carb diet? There is no standard definition. The DRI's (Dietary Reference Intakes) recommend a *minimum* of 130 grams of total carbohydrate daily, that is, the minimum required for normal functioning of the brain and nervous system. Because the long-term effects of following a very low-carbohydrate diet are still unknown, we would not advocate eating fewer than 130 grams of carbohydrate daily, which can be considered "low" compared to the Dietary Reference Intake-recommended optimal intake amount of 45—65% of total calories from carbohydrates (45—65% of a 2000-calorie diet is 225—325 grams of carbohydrate).

The following sample menu is an example of an eating plan based on 130 grams of carbohydrate a day. (Italic indicates recipe in book.)

MEAL	ONE SERVING	PAGE NO.	NET CARBS	MEAL TOTALS
BREAKFAST	fresh orange		8	
	Breakfast Pizza	64	20	**28**
LUNCH	*El Paso Bean & Corn Salad*	48	27	
	Fresh Cantaloupe (1½ cups)		17	
	Sugar-free Lemonade		0	**44**
DINNER	*Portobello Mushrooms with Sautéed Vegetables and Blue Cheese Polenta*	117	29	
	Tossed Salad w/ Dressing		12	
	Low-Carb Ice Cream (½ cup) with strawberries (¾ cup)		17	
	Iced Tea		0	**58**
DAILY TOTALS				**130**

NET CARBS AND THE GLYCEMIC INDEX

New research in carbohydrate metabolism indicates that not all carbs are created equal. We also took "Net Carbs" and the "Glycemic Index" into account when we developed the recipes for *Low-Carb Vegetarian Cooking.*

The net carb is based on the belief that fiber sources of carbohydrate are not absorbed by the body and therefore are calorie-free, do not affect blood sugars, and do not contribute to weight gain. Since this is the case, fiber carbs can be subtracted from the total carbohydrate count of a recipe or food. The total carbohydrates minus the fiber carbohydrates leaves the "net" carbs available to the body. This difference between the total carbs and fiber is also known as "impact carbs," as these are the carbs that have an "impact" on the body. In this book we chose to use the term "net carbs," and this figure is provided with each recipe.

In addition, some carbohydrates increase blood sugar faster than other carbohydrates. The speed at which carbs are converted to blood sugar has been measured for some foods and is called the glycemic index (G.I.). The higher the G. I. number, the faster the carbs change to blood sugar. With high G.I. foods, the rapid rise in blood sugar causes insulin, a hormone produced in the pancreas, to peak, resulting in a rapid drop in blood sugar, which then leads to hunger, snacking, and overeating. The lower the G.I. number, the slower the carbs change into blood sugar and the less insulin is released, which results in less overeating.

White bread and white sugar get the highest G. I. value of 100. When you choose carbohydrate foods to complement recipes in this book, pick those with both low net carbs and low glycemic indexes. For example, if rice is served with a stir-fry recipe, brown rice would be the better choice since it has a G.I. of 50 compared to 56 for white rice. Or, if breakfast includes fruit, $^1/_2$ of a grapefruit has a lower G.I. than a banana.

The chart below lists a variety of commonly consumed foods with known glycemic indexes. The total carbohydrate, net carbohydrate, and glycemic index are listed for each. All values are for 100-gram amounts, which is approximately $^1/_2$ cup.

CARBOHYDRATE, NET CARBOHYDRATE, AND GLYCEMIC INDEX FOR COMMON FOODS

FOOD ITEM (100 GMS)	TOTAL CARBS (GMS)	NET CARBS (GMS)	GLYCEMIC INDEX (G.I.)
Apples	15.2	12.5	38
Apple Juice	11.7	11.6	40
Apricots	11.1	8.7	57
Bananas	23.4	21.0	52
Cantaloupe	8.4	7.6	65
Cherries	13.7	11.4	22
Grapefruit	7.7	6.4	25
Grapefruit Juice	9.2	9.1	48
Grapes	17.8	16.8	43
Oranges	11.8	9.4	42
Orange Juice	10.4	10.2	52
Peaches	11.1	9.1	42
Pears	15.1	12.7	38
Strawberries	7.0	4.7	40
Watermelon	7.2	6.7	72
Baked Beans	19.4	14.6	56
Kidney Beans	22.8	16.4	28
Lentils	20.1	10.4	26
Macaroni	28.4	27.1	47
Spaghetti	28.3	26.6	38
Pearled Barley, dry	77.7	62.1	29
All Bran Cereal	74.2	41.9	38
100% Whole-Grain Bread	41.2	26.5	51
Cornmeal, dry	77.7	70.3	69
Couscous, cooked	23.2	21.8	65
Oat Bran	66.2	50.8	55
Brown Rice, cooked	23.0	21.2	50
White Rice, cooked	28.2	27.8	56
Shredded Wheat	82.5	71.6	75

CHOOSE THE RIGHT INGREDIENTS

In developing recipes for this book, we were careful to select carbs with low glycemic indexes and have, where possible, used whole-grain pastas rather than white semolina flour pastas, whole wheat flour rather than all-purpose white flour, brown rice instead of white rice, and brown sugar or sugar substitute instead of white sugar.

Fat in a meal helps control weight by increasing the time it takes to digest that meal, thus delaying the onset of hunger. Fat works with the low-glycemic foods to help improve your sense of fullness and satisfaction, which is why the recipes in this book mostly use full-fat products. As a bonus, full-fat foods frequently have fewer carbohydrates than the lower-fat products.

Also, we chose to use natural fats in order to avoid trans-fatty acids, which are associated with LDL ("bad") cholesterol and heart disease. On the other hand, monounsaturated fats, the kind associated with HDL ("good") cholesterol, are considered healthy for the heart. These include olive oil, flax seeds and their oil, and walnuts and their oil. Olive oil and canola oil are used for most of the recipes in this book because of their monounsaturated fat content.

NUTRITIONAL DATA

Low-Carb Vegetarian Cooking is an invaluable guide to preparing healthy, low-carbohydrate vegetarian meals for your family. The delicious recipes can be used successfully with any low-carbohydrate diet plan already being followed.

We have provided nutritional information for each recipe in this book, but remember that nutritional data are not always infallible. The nutritional analyses were derived using computer software highly regarded by nutritionists and dietitians, but they are meant only as guidelines. Figures are based on actual laboratory values of ingredients, so results may vary slightly, depending on the brand or manufacturer of an ingredient used.

Ingredients noted as "optional" or "to taste" or "as garnish" are not included in the nutritional analyses. When alternate choices or amounts of ingredients are given, the ingredient or amount listed first was used for analysis. Similarly, data is based on the first number of servings shown, where a range is given. Nutritional analyses are also based on the cooking instructions given; other procedures will invalidate data.

Other factors that can affect the accuracy of nutritional data include variability in sizes, weights, and measures of fruits, vegetables, and other foods. There is also a possible 20 percent error factor in the nutritional labeling of prepared foods.

If you have any health problems that require strict dietary requirements, it is important to consult a physician or registered dietitian before using recipes in this or any other cookbook. Also, if you are a diabetic or require a diet that restricts calories, fat, or sodium, remember that nutritional data might be accurate for the recipe as written but not for the food you cooked due to the variables explained above.

Recipes are coded so you can quickly tell whether they are vegan, lacto-ovo vegetarian, lacto-vegetarian, or ovo-vegetarian.

- v   *Vegan*—Recipes contain only plant-based food, with no dairy products or eggs.
- LO *Lacto-Ovo Vegetarian*—Recipes contain dairy products and eggs.
- L   *Lacto-Vegetarian*—Recipes contain dairy products but no eggs.
- o   *Ovo-Vegetarian*—Recipes contain eggs, but no dairy products.

We hope you'll enjoy the delicious low-carb recipes we've created for you. It's easy to stay with your plan for diet and exercise if the food you eat tastes wonderful, isn't it?

—LINDA R. YOAKAM, M.S., R.D.

CHAPTER ONE

Soups

Cream of Artichoke and Mushroom Soup with Parmesan Toast

L | *Shiitake or cremini mushrooms can be substituted for the portobello mushrooms.*

4 SERVINGS (ABOUT 1 CUP EACH)

- $3/4$ cup chopped portobello mushrooms
- 2 tablespoons finely chopped onion
- 1 tablespoon butter
- 1 tablespoon all-purpose flour
- 3 cups reduced-fat milk
- $1/4$ cup instant nonfat dry milk
- 1 vegetable bouillon cube
- 1 package (9 ounces) frozen artichoke hearts, thawed, finely chopped

Salt and white pepper, to taste

Paprika, as garnish

- 4 slices Parmesan Toast (double recipe) (see p. 76)

Sauté mushrooms and onion in butter in medium saucepan until tender, about 5 minutes. Stir in flour; cook 1 minute. Stir in milk, dry milk, and bouillon cube; heat to boiling, stirring constantly.

Stir in artichoke hearts; reduce heat and simmer, uncovered, 5 minutes. Season to taste with salt and white pepper. Pour soup into bowls and sprinkle with paprika; serve with Parmesan Toast.

(see p. 76)

PER SERVING

Net Carbohydrate (gm): 17.4
Calories: 261.3
Fat (gm): 9.8

Saturated Fat (gm): 4.2
Cholesterol (mg): 27.9
Sodium (mg): 645

Protein (gm): 16.3
Carbohydrate (gm): 30.0

Kidney Bean and Cabbage Soup

☐ *The beans that are lowest in carbohydrates include kidney, black, and pinto—use any of these in this nutritious soup.*

6 SERVINGS (ABOUT 1½ CUPS EACH)

    3 cups thinly sliced or chopped cabbage
  ⅓ cup coarsely chopped onion
    3 cloves garlic, minced
    1 teaspoon crushed caraway seeds
    1 tablespoon olive oil
    1 quart vegetable broth
    2 cups drained, rinsed, canned kidney beans
    6 ounces low-carb whole wheat macaroni
      Salt and pepper, to taste

Sauté cabbage, onion, garlic, and caraway seeds in oil in large saucepan until cabbage begins to wilt, 8 to 10 minutes.

Add broth and beans to saucepan; heat to boiling. Stir in pasta; reduce heat and simmer, uncovered, until pasta is al dente, 10 to 15 minutes. Season to taste with salt and pepper.

PER SERVING

Net Carbohydrate (gm): 23.3	Saturated Fat (gm): 0.4	Protein (gm): 14.0
Calories: 233.2	Cholesterol (mg): 0.0	Carbohydrate (gm): 36.7
Fat (gm): 3.5	Sodium (mg): 696	

Cream of Broccoli Soup with Mushroom Toast

L *For convenience, make the mushroom mixture for the Mushroom Toast in advance; refrigerate up to 2 days. Heat before spreading on toast.*

6 SERVINGS (ABOUT 1 CUP EACH)

$^1/_2$ cup chopped onion

3 cloves garlic, minced

1 tablespoon olive oil

2 pounds broccoli, cut into 1-inch pieces

$^1/_2$ teaspoon dried thyme leaves

$^1/_8$ teaspoon ground nutmeg

$3^1/_2$ cups vegetable broth

$^1/_2$ cup instant nonfat dry milk

$^1/_2$ cup whipping cream or half-and-half

Salt and white pepper, to taste

6 tablespoons sour cream

2–3 teaspoons lemon juice

Mushroom Toast (recipe follows)

Sauté onion and garlic in oil in large saucepan until tender, 3 to 5 minutes. Stir in broccoli, thyme, and nutmeg; cook 2 minutes longer.

Add broth to saucepan; heat to boiling. Reduce heat and simmer, covered, until broccoli is very tender, about 10 minutes.

Process soup and dry milk in food processor or blender until smooth. Return soup to saucepan; add cream and cook over medium heat until hot. Season to taste with salt and white pepper. Pour soup into bowls. Mix sour cream and lemon juice; swirl about 1 tablespoon of mixture into each bowl of soup. Serve with Mushroom Toast.

Mushroom Toast

MAKES 6 PIECES

   1 cup finely chopped mushrooms

   2 tablespoons finely chopped onion

   1 tablespoon olive oil

   2 pinches dried thyme leaves

     Salt and pepper, to taste

   6 slices low-carb whole wheat bread, toasted, halved

Sauté mushrooms and onion in oil in small skillet until mushrooms are tender, 3 to 4 minutes; stir in thyme and season to taste with salt and pepper. Spread mixture on toast slices.

PER SERVING

Net Carbohydrate (gm): 20.9	Saturated Fat (gm): 6.9	Protein (gm): 12.3
Calories: 296.9	Cholesterol (mg): 33.7	Carbohydrate (gm): 28.9
Fat (gm): 16.9	Sodium (mg): 496	

Cream of Cauliflower Soup

L *Serve this soup with Parmesan Croutons (see p. 19) for a lively accent. Make the croutons up to a week in advance and store in an airtight container at room temperature.*

4 SERVINGS (ABOUT 1½ CUPS EACH)

- ½ cup chopped onion
- 2 cloves garlic, minced
- 1 tablespoon butter
- 2 tablespoons all-purpose flour
- 3½ cups vegetable broth
- 3 cups cauliflower florets
- 1 cup cubed, peeled Idaho potato
- ¼ cup light cream
- ¼ cup instant nonfat dry milk
- 1 cup (4 ounces) shredded Cheddar cheese
- Salt and white pepper, to taste
- Ground mace or nutmeg, as garnish

Sauté onion and garlic in butter in large saucepan until tender, about 5 minutes. Stir in flour; cook 1 minute longer. Add broth, cauliflower, and potato; heat to boiling. Reduce heat and simmer, covered, until vegetables are tender, 10 to 15 minutes.

Remove about half the vegetables from the soup with a slotted spoon and reserve. Process remaining soup in food processor or blender until smooth. Return soup to saucepan; stir in reserved vegetables, cream, dry milk, and cheese. Cook over low heat until cheese is melted, 3 to 4 minutes, stirring frequently. Season to taste with salt and white pepper.

Pour soup into bowls; sprinkle lightly with mace.

VARIATIONS:

Fennel Bisque with Walnuts—Make soup as above, substituting the white part of a leek for the onion, and sliced fennel for the cauliflower. Complete soup as above, omitting the Cheddar cheese. Ladle soup into bowls; sprinkle with 3 ounces crumbled blue cheese and $1/4$ cup chopped toasted walnuts.

Cream of Turnip Soup—Make soup as above, substituting chopped turnips for the cauliflower, and Swiss, Gouda, or Havarti cheese for the Cheddar; add $1/2$ teaspoon dried thyme leaves.

··

PER SERVING

Net Carbohydrate (gm): 20.9 Saturated Fat (gm): 9.4   Protein (gm): 12.7
Calories: 288.8   Cholesterol (mg): 48.4   Carbohydrate (gm): 24.8
Fat (gm): 15.9   Sodium (mg): 655

Eggplant Soup with Red Pepper Swirl and Feta Toast

L *For indoor cooking, eggplant can be oven roasted. Pierce the eggplant in several places with a fork and place them in a baking pan. Bake at 350 degrees until the eggplant is soft, 45 to 50 minutes.*

4 SERVINGS (ABOUT 1 CUP EACH)

>   2 medium eggplant (about 2^1/$_2$ pounds)
> ^{3}/$_4$ cup chopped onion
> ^{1}/$_4$ cup chopped green bell pepper
>   2 cloves garlic, minced
>   1 tablespoon extra-virgin olive oil
>   4–5 cups vegetable broth
>   Salt and white pepper, to taste
> ^{1}/$_2$ cup roasted red bell pepper, pureed
>   Feta Toast (recipe follows)

Pierce eggplant in several places with fork; grill over medium hot coals, turning frequently, until very soft, about 30 minutes. Cool until warm enough to handle; cut each eggplant in half, scoop out pulp, and chop coarsely.

Sauté onion, green pepper, and garlic in oil in large saucepan until tender, 5 to 8 minutes. Add broth and eggplant to saucepan; heat to boiling. Reduce heat and simmer, covered, 10 minutes.

Process soup in food processor or blender until smooth. Season to taste with salt and white pepper. Refrigerate until chilled, 4 to 6 hours.

Pour soup into bowls; swirl 2 tablespoons roasted pepper puree into each bowl. Serve with Feta Toast.

Feta Toast

MAKES 12 PIECES

6 slices low-carb or thin-sliced whole wheat bread
1 cup (4 ounces) crumbled feta cheese

Sprinkle bread slices with cheese; broil 4 inches from heat source until cheese is softened, 2 to 3 minutes. Cut bread slices diagonally into halves.

PER SERVING
Net Carbohydrate (gm): 30.4   Saturated Fat (gm): 6.8   Protein (gm): 18.3
Calories: 388.0   Cholesterol (mg): 37.4   Carbohydrate (gm): 47.4
Fat (gm): 16.8   Sodium (mg): 1780

Cream of Mushroom Soup

Creamy and rich, this soup bears resemblance to the favorite-brand canned soup we fondly remember!

4 SERVINGS (ABOUT 1¼ CUPS EACH)

- 1 pound mushrooms
- 2 tablespoons butter, divided
- 1 cup chopped onion
- 2½ cups vegetable broth
- 2 cups reduced-fat milk
- ½ cup instant nonfat dry milk
- ½ cup light cream or half-and-half
- 2 tablespoons plus 2 teaspoons cornstarch
- Salt and pepper, to taste
- Parsley leaves, minced, as garnish

Slice enough mushroom caps to make 2 cups; finely chop stems and remaining mushrooms. Sauté sliced mushrooms in 1 tablespoon butter in large saucepan until browned, about 5 minutes; remove and reserve. Sauté onion and chopped mushrooms in remaining 1 tablespoon butter in saucepan until onion is tender, about 5 minutes.

Add broth, milk, and dry milk to saucepan, mixing well; heat to boiling. Mix cream and cornstarch; whisk into boiling mixture. Boil, whisking constantly, until thickened, about 1 minute. Stir in reserved sliced mushrooms. Season to taste with salt and pepper. Serve in bowls; sprinkle with parsley.

PER SERVING

Net Carbohydrate (gm): 23.9
Calories: 279.0
Fat (gm): 15.1

Saturated Fat (gm): 7.9
Cholesterol (mg): 47.3
Sodium (mg): 773

Protein (gm): 11.9
Carbohydrate (gm): 25.8

Two-Season Squash and Bean Soup with Gruyere Melts

L *Winter and summer squash are combined with beans in this flavorful soup.*

6 SERVINGS (ABOUT 1¼ CUPS EACH)

1 cup chopped onion

2 cloves garlic, minced

2 teaspoons olive oil

3 cups vegetable broth

2 cups cubed, seeded, peeled butternut or hubbard squash

2 cups sliced zucchini

1 can (28 ounces) reduced-sodium whole tomatoes, undrained, chopped

1 can (15 ounces) pinto or black beans, rinsed, drained

3 tablespoons minced parsley

1 bay leaf

1 teaspoon low-sodium Worcestershire sauce

1 teaspoon dried marjoram leaves

½ teaspoon dried rosemary leaves

Salt and pepper, to taste

6 slices low-carb whole wheat bread

1¼ cups (5 ounces) shredded Gruyere or Swiss cheese

Sauté onion and garlic in oil in large saucepan until tender, about 5 minutes. Add remaining ingredients, except salt and pepper, bread, and cheese. Heat to boiling; reduce heat and simmer, covered, until squash is tender, about 25 minutes. Discard bay leaf; season to taste with salt and pepper.

Sprinkle bread slices with cheese; broil 6 inches from heat source until cheese is melted, 2 to 3 minutes. Serve with soup.

···

PER SERVING

Net Carbohydrate (gm): 29.0 Saturated Fat (gm): 5.7 Protein (gm): 19.2

Calories: 336.6 Cholesterol (mg): 30.8 Carbohydrate (gm): 39.3

Fat (gm): 13.3 Sodium (mg): 690

Creamy Tomato-Vegetable Soup with Cheese and Spinach Squares

L-O *Cut green beans, broccoli florets, yellow summer squash, and sugar-snap peas are other vegetable options for this soup— enjoy the season's bounty!*

6 SERVINGS (ABOUT 1⅓ CUPS EACH)

   ⅔ cup finely chopped onion
   ⅔ cup chopped green bell pepper
   ½ cup chopped celery
    1 large garlic clove, minced
    1 tablespoon butter
    2 tablespoons all-purpose flour
    1 quart vegetable broth
    2 cups diced zucchini
1 ½ cups small cauliflower florets
   ¼ cup dry sherry, optional
   ¼ cup finely chopped parsley
    1 teaspoon dried basil leaves
   ¼ teaspoon dried thyme leaves
    1 can (8 ounces) tomato sauce
   ¾ cup whipping cream or half-and-half
      Salt and cayenne pepper, to taste
      Cheese and Spinach Squares (recipe follows)

Sauté onion, bell pepper, celery, and garlic in butter in large saucepan until onion is tender, about 5 minutes. Sprinkle with flour and cook 1 minute longer. Add broth, zucchini, cauliflower, sherry, and herbs; heat to boiling. Reduce heat and simmer, covered, until vegetables are tender, about 10 minutes.

Stir in tomato sauce and cream; simmer 2 to 3 minutes. Season to taste with salt and cayenne pepper. Serve with Cheese and Spinach squares.

Cheese and Spinach Squares

MAKES 6 SERVINGS (12 PIECES)

1–2 tablespoons unseasoned dry bread crumbs

1 cup cottage cheese

$3/4$ cup (3 ounces) shredded Cheddar cheese

1 egg

3 tablespoons all-purpose flour

$1/2$ package (10 ounce-size) frozen chopped spinach, thawed, well-drained

$1/4$ cup thinly sliced green onions and tops

$1/4$ cup chopped roasted red bell pepper or pimiento

$1/8$ teaspoon ground nutmeg

$1/2$ teaspoon pepper

Coat bottom and sides of greased 8 x 8-inch baking pan with bread crumbs.

Combine cheeses, egg and flour in bowl; stir in remaining ingredients and mix well. Pour into prepared pan and bake at 350 degrees until set and lightly browned, 35 to 40 minutes. Cool 10 minutes before cutting into squares.

PER SERVING
Net Carbohydrate (gm): 16.6
Calories: 322.3
Fat (gm): 21.2

Saturated Fat (gm): 12.3
Cholesterol (mg): 101.8
Sodium (mg): 815

Protein (gm): 14.2
Carbohydrate (gm): 21.3

Tangy Zucchini Soup with Artichoke Cheese Spread

L-O *Artichoke Cheese Spread also makes a great party appetizer.*
Make up to 3 days in advance, and refrigerate.

4 SERVINGS (ABOUT 1½ CUPS EACH)

- 3 cups vegetable broth
- 2 cups diced zucchini
- ⅔ cup finely chopped onion
- ½ cup diced, peeled potato
- 2 tablespoons chopped fresh parsley
- 1 small clove garlic, minced
- ¼ teaspoon dry mustard
- Dash cayenne pepper
- ½ cup instant nonfat dry milk
- ½ cup buttermilk
- ½ cup whipping cream or half-and-half
- Salt and white pepper, to taste
- Thinly sliced zucchini, as garnish
- Artichoke Cheese Spread (recipe follows)
- 4 slices low-carb whole wheat bread, toasted, halved

Combine broth, zucchini, onion, potato, parsley, garlic, mustard, and cayenne pepper in large saucepan; heat to boiling. Reduce heat and simmer, covered, until potato is very tender, about 15 minutes; stir in dry milk.

Process in blender or food processor until smooth; transfer to serving bowl. Stir in buttermilk and cream; season to taste with salt and white pepper. Refrigerate until chilled.

Pour soup into bowls and garnish with sliced zucchini. Spread Artichoke Cheese Spread on toast and serve with soup.

Artichoke Cheese Spread

MAKES ABOUT 1 CUP

$^1/_2$ package (8 ounce-size) cream cheese, softened
$^1/_2$ can (14 ounce-size) artichoke hearts, drained, finely chopped
$^1/_4$ cup mayonnaise
$^1/_4$ cup chopped red bell pepper
1 clove garlic, minced

Beat all ingredients until smooth.

PER SERVING

Net Carbohydrate (gm): 28.4   Saturated Fat (gm): 15.0   Protein (gm): 14.5
Calories: 488.5   Cholesterol (mg): 80.3   Carbohydrate (gm): 34.2
Fat (gm): 34.2   Sodium (mg): 883

Lentil-Vegetable Soup

L · *Open-face cream cheese, cucumber, and dill sandwiches make the perfect accents for this flavorful soup.*

4 SERVINGS (ABOUT 1½ CUPS EACH)

$\frac{1}{2}$ cup chopped onion

$\frac{1}{2}$ cup chopped carrot

$\frac{1}{2}$ cup chopped celery

1 clove garlic, minced

$\frac{1}{2}$ teaspoon dried thyme leaves

$\frac{1}{8}$–$\frac{1}{4}$ teaspoon red pepper flakes

1 tablespoon olive oil

$\frac{1}{2}$ cup dried lentils

1 quart vegetable broth

1 can (14$\frac{1}{2}$ ounces) stewed tomatoes, undrained

Salt and pepper, to taste

4 slices low-carb whole wheat bread

$\frac{1}{2}$ package (8 ounce-size) cream cheese, softened

$\frac{1}{4}$ cup cucumber slices

$\frac{1}{2}$ teaspoon dried dill weed

Sauté onion, carrot, celery, garlic, thyme, and red pepper flakes in oil in large saucepan until onion is browned, about 5 minutes. Stir in lentils and broth; heat to boiling. Reduce heat and simmer, covered, 30 minutes, or until lentils are just tender. Add tomatoes and liquid; simmer, uncovered, 10 minutes. Season to taste with salt and pepper.

Spread bread slices with cream cheese; top with cucumber slices and sprinkle with dill weed. Serve with soup.

PER SERVING

Net Carbohydrate (gm): 22.4

Calories: 347.0

Fat (gm): 15.9

Saturated Fat (gm): 6.7

Cholesterol (mg): 31.2

Sodium (mg): 1002

Protein (gm): 15.4

Carbohydrate (gm): 39.1

Tempeh Pasta Soup

o *Tempeh contains about 2 times more protein than tofu, making it a nutritious choice for this soup.*

4 SERVINGS (ABOUT 1¼ CUPS EACH)

    2 cups sliced celery, including some leaves
    1 cup sliced carrots
    1 cup sliced onion
    1 tablespoon canola oil
 3½ cups vegetable broth
    1 package (8 ounces) tempeh or firm tofu, coarsely chopped
    1 teaspoon dried marjoram leaves
    1 bay leaf
    1 cup uncooked low-carb pasta shells
    1 tablespoon minced parsley
      Salt and pepper, to taste

Sauté celery, carrots, and onion in oil in large saucepan until crisp-tender, 5 to 8 minutes. Add broth, tempeh, and herbs to saucepan; heat to boiling. Reduce heat and simmer, covered, until vegetables are tender, about 10 minutes.

Heat soup to boiling; add pasta. Reduce heat and simmer, uncovered, until pasta is tender, 7 to 10 minutes. Discard bay leaf. Stir in parsley and season to taste with salt and pepper.

PER SERVING

Net Carbohydrate (gm): 23.9	Saturated Fat (gm): 1.6	Protein (gm): 19.6
Calories: 295.8	Cholesterol (mg): 0.0	Carbohydrate (gm): 32.4
Fat (gm): 10.7	Sodium (mg): 1015	

Garden Minestrone with Parmesan Croutons

L-O   *If desired, stir 1 cup torn kale or lightly packed baby spinach leaves into the soup during the last 2 to 3 minutes of cooking time.*

6 SERVINGS (ABOUT 1⅔ CUPS EACH)

    ½ cup sliced carrot
    ½ cup sliced green onions and tops
    ½ cup chopped celery
    ½ cup sliced fennel bulb or celery
    2 cloves garlic, minced
    1 tablespoon olive oil
    5 cups vegetable broth
    1 can (19 ounces) garbanzo beans, rinsed, drained
    1 cup snap peas
    1 cup sliced zucchini
    1 cup broccoli florets
    1 cup halved cherry tomatoes
    ¼ cup finely chopped parsley
    ¾–1 teaspoon dried basil leaves
    ¾–1 teaspoon dried oregano leaves
    1 ounce uncooked low-carb whole wheat macaroni
      Salt and pepper, to taste
      Parmesan Croutons (recipe follows)

Sauté carrot, green onions, celery, fennel, and garlic in oil in Dutch oven until onion is tender, 5 to 8 minutes. Add remaining ingredients, except salt, pepper, and Parmesan Croutons and heat to boiling. Reduce heat and simmer, covered, until vegetables and pasta are tender, 10 to 15 minutes. Season to taste with salt and pepper.

Pour soup into bowls; sprinkle with Parmesan croutons.

Parmesan Croutons

MAKES ABOUT 1½ CUPS

1½ cups cubed day-old low-carb whole wheat bread
  (½-inch cubes)
  Vegetable cooking spray
2 tablespoons grated Parmesan cheese

Spray bread cubes with cooking spray; toss with Parmesan cheese. Arrange bread cubes in single layer on jelly roll pan; bake at 375 degrees until browned, 8 to 10 minutes, stirring occasionally. Cool.

PER SERVING

Net Carbohydrate (gm): 29.5	Saturated Fat (gm): 0.7	Protein (gm): 11.2
Calories: 240.3	Cholesterol (mg): 1.5	Carbohydrate (gm): 39.3
Fat (gm): 5.3	Sodium (mg): 791	

"Meatball" and Vegetable Soup

The perfect soup when you expect a crowd! The tasty "meatballs" are made with vegetable protein crumbles; packaged soy meatballs can be substituted.

12 SERVINGS (ABOUT 2 CUPS EACH)

8 ounces acorn, hubbard or butternut squash, peeled, seeded, cut into scant $3/4$-inch cubes

$1/2$ cup chopped onion

2 cloves garlic, minced

1 tablespoon olive oil

5 cups vegetable broth

1 can (16 ounces) reduced-sodium diced tomatoes, undrained

1 can (15 ounces) garbanzo beans, rinsed, drained

$1/2$ cup frozen peas

1 teaspoon dried Italian seasoning

"Meatballs" (recipe follows)

4 ounces uncooked low-carb whole wheat rotini

Salt and pepper, to taste

Chopped fresh basil or fresh parsley, as garnish

Sauté squash, onion, and garlic in oil in Dutch oven until onion is tender, about 5 minutes. Add broth, tomatoes with liquid, beans, peas, and Italian seasoning; heat to boiling. Reduce heat and simmer, covered, 10 minutes.

Heat soup to boiling; add "Meatballs" and pasta. Reduce heat and simmer, uncovered, until pasta is tender, 7 to 10 minutes. Season to taste with salt and pepper.

Pour soup into bowls; sprinkle with basil.

"Meatballs"

MAKES 36

- 1 slice low-carb whole wheat bread
- 1 package (16 ounces) frozen pre-browned vegetable protein crumbles, thawed
- 3 eggs, lightly beaten
- 3 cloves garlic, minced
- 3 tablespoons grated Parmesan
- 2 teaspoons dried Italian seasoning
- 1/2 teaspoon fennel seeds, crushed

Process bread in food processor or blender until the texture of fine crumbs. Combine crumbs with remaining ingredients, mashing protein crumbles lightly with fork. Form mixture into 36 balls.

PER SERVING

Net Carbohydrate (gm): 18.7	Saturated Fat (gm): 0.8	Protein (gm): 17.2
Calories: 213.2	Cholesterol (mg): 54.0	Carbohydrate (gm): 27.5
Fat (gm): 4.1	Sodium (mg): 682	

Hot Sour Soup

□ o *The contrast in hot and sour flavors makes this Mandarin soup
a unique offering. The hot chili sesame oil and Sour Sauce are
intensely flavored, so use sparingly.*

6 SERVINGS (ABOUT 1 CUP EACH)

$^1/_2$ ounce dried shiitake mushrooms

$^3/_4$ cup boiling water

1 quart vegetable broth

$^1/_2$ cup bamboo shoots

$^1/_4$ cup distilled white vinegar

2 tablespoons reduced-sodium tamari soy sauce

1 tablespoon finely chopped gingerroot

1 teaspoon brown sugar

1 tablespoon cornstarch

3 tablespoons water

2 cups (8 ounces) cubed tempeh or extra-firm tofu

Salt, cayenne, and black pepper, to taste

2 eggs, lightly beaten

1–2 teaspoons dark sesame oil

Sliced green onion, as garnish

12–18 drops hot chili sesame oil or Szechwan chili sauce

Sour Sauce (recipe follows)

Combine mushrooms and boiling water in small bowl; let stand until
mushrooms are softened, 15 to 20 minutes. Strain liquid through fine
strainer and reserve. Slice mushrooms, discarding tough stems.

Combine broth, mushrooms and reserved liquid, bamboo shoots, vinegar,
soy sauce, gingerroot, and sugar in large saucepan; heat to boiling. Reduce
heat and simmer, uncovered, 10 minutes. Heat soup to boiling; mix cornstarch and water and stir into soup. Boil until thickened, about 1 minute,
stirring constantly.

Stir tempeh into soup; simmer, covered, 5 minutes. Season to taste with salt, cayenne, and black pepper. Just before serving, stir eggs slowly into soup; stir in sesame oil.

Pour soup into bowls and sprinkle with green onion; add hot chili oil and Sour Sauce as desired.

Sour Sauce

MAKES ABOUT ⅓ CUP

> 3 tablespoons distilled white vinegar
> 1 tablespoon reduced-sodium tamari soy sauce
> 2 tablespoons packed light brown sugar

Mix all ingredients.

PER SERVING
Net Carbohydrate (gm): 13.9   Saturated Fat (gm): 1.1   Protein (gm): 12.2
Calories: 185.0   Cholesterol (mg): 70.5   Carbohydrate (gm): 19.1
Fat (gm): 6.8   Sodium (mg): 642

SOUPS • 23

Asian Mushroom Soup with Noodles

| o |

Two kind of mushrooms contribute rich flavor to this soup. Soba noodles can be substituted for the low-carb whole wheat noodles.

6 SERVINGS (ABOUT 1½ CUPS EACH)

- 3 cups boiling water
- 1 ounce dried shiitake mushrooms
- 2 pounds cremini mushrooms, sliced, divided
- ½ cup minced onion
- 1 clove garlic, minced
- ¼ teaspoon dried thyme leaves
- 2 tablespoons canola oil
- 1 quart vegetable broth
- ½ cup dry white wine or vegetable broth
- 3 ounces uncooked low-carb whole wheat linguini or fettuccini
- 1 cup trimmed snow peas
- ⅓ cup thinly sliced radishes
- 2 tablespoons finely chopped fresh parsley
- 1 tablespoon red wine vinegar
- Salt and pepper, to taste

Pour boiling water over dried mushrooms in bowl and let stand until softened, about 15 minutes. Strain liquid through fine strainer and reserve. Coarsely chop shiitake mushrooms and stems.

Sauté shiitake mushrooms, half of the cremini mushrooms, onion, garlic, and thyme in oil in large saucepan until soft, 5 to 8 minutes. Add broth, wine, and reserved mushroom liquid; heat to boiling. Reduce heat and simmer, covered, 30 minutes.

Strain soup, discarding mushrooms. Add remaining cremini mushrooms, pasta, snow peas, radishes, parsley, and vinegar; simmer, uncovered, until pasta is cooked, about 8 minutes. Season to taste with salt and pepper.

PER SERVING

Net Carbohydrate (gm): 14.0	Saturated Fat (gm): 0.3	Protein (gm): 12.3
Calories: 198.6	Cholesterol (mg): 0.0	Carbohydrate (gm): 22.1
Fat (gm): 5.2	Sodium (mg): 416	

Creamy Peanut Butter Soup

L

This soup will tempt peanut butter lovers! Pureed beans contribute rich texture and added nutrition without detracting from the great peanut flavor.

4 SERVINGS (ABOUT 1½ CUPS EACH)

¹/₂ cup chopped onion

¹/₂ cup chopped carrot

¹/₂ cup sliced celery

¹/₂ cup sliced leek (white part only)

2 cloves garlic, minced

1 tablespoon canola oil

3 cups vegetable broth

1 can (15 ounces) pinto beans rinsed, drained

¹/₂ cup creamy peanut butter

¹/₂ cup light cream or reduced-fat milk

³/₄–1 teaspoon teaspoon curry powder

2–3 teaspoons lemon juice

2–3 dashes red pepper sauce

Salt, cayenne, and black pepper, to taste

Thinly sliced green onions, as garnish

Sauté onion, carrot, celery, leek, and garlic in oil in large saucepan until onion is tender, about 5 minutes. Add broth and beans and heat to boiling; reduce heat and simmer, covered, until vegetables are tender, 10 to 15 minutes.

Process soup and peanut butter in food processor or blender until smooth. Return soup to saucepan; stir in cream and curry powder. Heat over medium heat until hot; season to taste with lemon juice, red pepper sauce, salt, cayenne, and black pepper. Serve in bowls; sprinkle with green onions.

....

PER SERVING

Net Carbohydrate (gm): 25.5   Saturated Fat (gm): 7.1   Protein (gm): 15.5

Calories: 420.1   Cholesterol (mg): 19.8   Carbohydrate (gm): 34.5

Fat (gm): 26.6   Sodium (mg): 845

Pasilla Black Bean Soup

L

For a hot and smoky flavor accent, add 1 to 2 teaspoons chopped canned chipotle peppers in adobo sauce to the soup with the broth.

4 SERVINGS (ABOUT 1½ CUPS EACH)

1 cup chopped onion

1 cup chopped carrots

1 jalapeño chili, chopped

4 cloves garlic, chopped

1 tablespoon olive oil

6 pasilla chilies, stems and seeds removed, torn into pieces

3/4 teaspoon dried oregano leaves

1/2 teaspoon ground cumin

1/4 teaspoon dried thyme leaves

1 quart vegetable broth

1 can (15 ounces) black beans, rinsed, drained

1 can (14½ ounces) diced tomatoes, undrained

Salt and pepper, to taste

3/4 cup (3 ounces) crumbled Mexican white cheese or feta cheese

Chopped fresh cilantro, as garnish

Sauté onion, carrots, jalapeño chili, and garlic in oil in large saucepan until onion is tender, about 5 minutes. Add pasilla chilies, oregano, cumin, and thyme; cook, covered, 5 minutes.

Add broth, beans, and tomatoes and liquid to saucepan; heat to boiling. Reduce heat and simmer, covered, 10 minutes. Process soup in food processor or blender until smooth. Season to taste with salt and pepper. Spoon into bowls and sprinkle with cheese and cilantro.

··

PER SERVING

Net Carbohydrate (gm): 29.0   Saturated Fat (gm): 4.5   Protein (gm): 13.3

Calories: 320.4   Cholesterol (mg): 22.3   Carbohydrate (gm): 36.7

Fat (gm): 12.1   Sodium (mg): 1235

Mexican Tortilla Soup with Black Bean Quesadillas

L   *A light, flavorful soup with South-of-the-Border flavors!*

4 SERVINGS (ABOUT 1²/₃ CUPS EACH)

        2 low-carb whole wheat tortillas, cut into 2 x ¹/₄-inch strips
          Vegetable cooking spray
        2 cups sliced carrots
        1 cup sliced red bell pepper
      ³/₄ cup sliced celery
      ¹/₃ cup sliced green onions and tops
        6 cloves garlic, minced
        1 small jalapeño chili, finely chopped
        1 tablespoon canola oil
    1¹/₂ quarts vegetable broth
  ¹/₂–³/₄ cup lime juice
      ¹/₂ teaspoon ground cumin
          Salt and pepper, to taste
        1 cup chopped tomato
      ¹/₂ cup chopped, seeded cucumber
      ¹/₂ cup chopped avocado
      ¹/₄ cup finely chopped cilantro
          Black Bean Quesadillas (recipe follows)

Spray tortilla strips with cooking spray, tossing lightly to coat. Cook in greased skillet over medium heat, tossing occasionally, until browned and crisp, about 5 minutes; reserve.

Sauté carrots, bell pepper, celery, green onions, garlic, and jalapeño chili in oil in large saucepan until lightly browned, about 5 minutes.

Add broth, lime juice, and cumin to saucepan; heat to boiling. Reduce heat and simmer, covered, until vegetables are tender, 10 to 15 minutes. Season to taste with salt and pepper.

Pour soup into bowls; add tomato, cucumber, and avocado to each bowl. Sprinkle with cilantro and tortilla strips. Serve with Black Bean Quesadillas.

Black Bean Quesadillas

MAKES 2 QUESADILLAS

$^1/_2$ can (15 ounce-size) black beans, rinsed, drained

$^1/_2$ cup (2 ounces) shredded Mexican cheese blend

$^1/_4$ cup mild or medium, salsa

2 tablespoons finely chopped cilantro

1 teaspoon finely chopped jalapeño chili

4 low-carb whole wheat tortillas (6-inch)

Mash beans slightly; mix with remaining ingredients, except tortillas.

Divide mixture on 2 tortillas; top with remaining tortillas. Cook in greased large skillet until browned, 2 to 3 minutes on each side. Cut into wedges.

PER SERVING

Net Carbohydrate (gm): 28.0	Saturated Fat (gm): 3.8	Protein (gm): 17.0
Calories: 346.3	Cholesterol (mg): 12.5	Carbohydrate (gm): 49.1
Fat (gm): 15.5	Sodium (mg): 1309	

Bean Gazpacho

L   *Pureed beans contribute nutritional value and a creamy texture to this delicious gazpacho.*

6 SERVINGS (ABOUT 1½ CUPS EACH)

$^3/_4$ cup ($^1/_2$ recipe) Parmesan Croutons (see p. 19)

$^3/_4$ teaspoon dried oregano leaves

2 cans (15½ ounces each) pinto beans, rinsed, drained

1 quart reduced-sodium tomato juice

3–4 tablespoons lime juice

2 teaspoons reduced-sodium Worcestershire sauce

1 cup thick and chunky mild or medium salsa

1 cup peeled, seeded, chopped cucumber

1 cup thinly sliced celery

$^1/_2$ cup sliced green onions and tops

$^1/_2$ cup chopped green bell pepper

2 teaspoons minced roasted garlic

$^1/_2$ small avocado, peeled, chopped

$^1/_2$ cup sour cream

Make Parmesan Croutons, deleting the Parmesan cheese and sprinkling the bread cubes with oregano leaves; bake according to recipe.

Process beans, tomato juice, lime juice, and Worcestershire sauce in food processor or blender until smooth; pour into large bowl. Mix in remaining ingredients, except avocado and sour cream. Refrigerate until chilled, 3 to 4 hours.

Mix avocado into soup and pour into bowls; garnish each with a dollop of sour cream and sprinkle with croutons.

PER SERVING

Net Carbohydrate (gm): 30.2	Saturated Fat (gm): 2.9	Protein (gm): 11.1
Calories: 263.1	Cholesterol (mg): 7.0	Carbohydrate (gm): 40.7
Fat (gm): 7.7	Sodium (mg): 820	

Tomatillo Soup with Cheese Quesadillas

| L | *Tomatillos are not really tomatoes, even though they look like it! The papery husks must be removed before using.* |

6 SERVINGS (ABOUT 1¼ CUPS EACH)

$^1/_2$ cup chopped onion

1–2 small jalapeño chilies, finely chopped

 2 cloves garlic, minced

 1 tablespoon olive or canola oil

 2 pounds tomatillos, husks removed, rinsed, quartered

 1 quart vegetable broth

$^1/_2$ cup half-and-half or reduced-fat milk

$^1/_3$ cup finely chopped fresh cilantro, divided

Salt and white pepper, to taste

Cheese Quesadillas (recipe follows)

Sauté onion, chilies, and garlic in oil in large saucepan until tender, about 5 minutes. Add tomatillos and broth and heat to boiling; reduce heat and simmer, covered, until tomatillos are very tender, 10 to 15 minutes.

Process soup in food processor or blender until smooth; stir in half-and-half and half of the cilantro. Season to taste with salt and white pepper. Refrigerate until chilled, 3 to 4 hours.

Pour soup into bowls; sprinkle with remaining cilantro. Serve with Cheese Quesadillas.

Cheese Quesadillas

MAKES 6 SERVINGS

6 low-carb or regular whole wheat tortillas

1 cup (4 ounces) shredded Monterey Jack cheese

1/4 cup thinly sliced green onions and tops

Sprinkle 3 of the tortillas with cheese and green onions; top with remaining tortillas. Cook over medium heat in greased large skillet until browned, 2 to 3 minutes on each side. Cut into wedges.

PER SERVING

Net Carbohydrate (gm): 15.6   Saturated Fat (gm): 5.3   Protein (gm): 15.0
Calories: 270.3   Cholesterol (mg): 27.4   Carbohydrate (gm): 32.8
Fat (gm): 15.5   Sodium (mg): 1084

Chili sin Carne

| L | *For a Southwest version of this chili, substitute black or pinto beans for the kidney beans and add 1 minced jalapeño chili. Garnish each serving with a sprinkling of finely chopped cilantro leaves.*

6 SERVINGS (ABOUT 1⅓ CUPS EACH)

$3/4$ cup chopped green bell pepper

$3/4$ cup sliced green onions and tops, divided

$1/2$ cup chopped onion

2 cloves garlic, minced

1 tablespoon olive oil

$1/2$ package (12-ounce size) frozen pre-browned vegetable protein crumbles

1–2 tablespoons chili powder

2 teaspoons ground cumin

1 teaspoon dried oregano leaves

$1/4$ teaspoon ground cloves

2 cans ($14^1/2$ ounces each) reduced-sodium diced tomatoes, undrained

$1/2$ can (6 ounce-size) reduced-sodium tomato paste

$3/4$ cup low-carb beer or water

1 tablespoon packed light brown sugar

2–3 teaspoons unsweetened cocoa

1 can (15 ounces) red kidney beans, rinsed, drained

Salt and pepper, to taste

$1/2$ cup (2 ounces) shredded Cheddar cheese

$1/2$ cup sour cream

Sauté bell pepper, $1/2$ cup green onions, onion, and garlic in oil in large saucepan until vegetables are tender, 5 to 8 minutes. Add vegetable protein crumbles, chili powder, cumin, oregano, and cloves; cook 1 to 2 minutes longer.

32 • LOW-CARB VEGETARIAN COOKING

Add tomatoes and liquid, tomato paste, beer, brown sugar, and cocoa to saucepan. Heat to boiling; reduce heat and simmer, covered, 45 minutes. Stir in beans and simmer, uncovered, to thicken if desired. Season to taste with salt and pepper.

Spoon chili into bowls; top with remaining $1/4$ cup green onions, cheese, and sour cream.

PER SERVING

Net Carbohydrate (gm): 20.8   Saturated Fat (gm): 4.5   Protein (gm): 15.3
Calories: 272.6   Cholesterol (mg): 17.2   Carbohydrate (gm): 32.0
Fat (gm): 9.8   Sodium (mg): 586

CHAPTER TWO

Salads

Summer Fruit Salad with Cilantro-Citrus Dressing

L *Take advantage of the season's ripest fruit for this salad.*

4 SERVINGS (ABOUT 1½ CUPS EACH)

- 1 cup sliced strawberries
- 1 cup blueberries
- 1 cup cantaloupe balls
- 1 cup sliced, peeled kiwi fruit
  Cilantro-Citrus Dressing (recipe follows), divided
- 3 cups cottage cheese
- 4 large bibb lettuce leaves
- 2 tablespoons grated orange rind

Combine fruit in a bowl; add ¼ cup Cilantro-Citrus Dressing and toss. Spoon fruit and cottage cheese onto lettuce-lined plates; drizzle remaining ¼ cup Cilantro-Citrus Dressing over cottage cheese and sprinkle with grated orange rind.

Cilantro-Citrus Dressing

MAKES ABOUT ½ CUP

- ¼ cup lime juice
- 2 tablespoons orange juice
- 2–3 tablespoons canola oil
- ¼ cup chopped cilantro
- 1 tablespoon honey

Mix all ingredients.

....

PER SERVING

Net Carbohydrate (gm): 27.6	Saturated Fat (gm): 3.0	Protein (gm): 25.0
Calories: 313	Cholesterol (mg): 13.6	Carbohydrate (gm): 31.4
Fat (gm): 10.7	Sodium (mg): 698	

12-Layer Garden Salad

L-O *Make this salad up to 24 hours in advance; toss just before serving.*

6 SERVINGS (ABOUT 1½ CUPS EACH)

    2 cups sliced spinach leaves
    2 cups thinly sliced red cabbage
    2 cups small broccoli florets
    6 ounces Cheddar cheese, cubed (½-inch)
    2 cups chopped iceberg lettuce
  ½ cup sliced or shredded carrot
  ½ cup sliced yellow or red bell pepper
  ½ cup thinly sliced small tomato
    1 cup cut green beans, cooked until crisp-tender, cooled
    1 can (15 ounces) dark red kidney beans, rinsed, drained
  ½ cup thinly sliced red onion
       Garlic Dressing (recipe follows)
  ¼ cup finely chopped fresh parsley
    3 hard-cooked eggs, cut into wedges

Layer spinach, cabbage, broccoli, cheese, lettuce, carrot, bell pepper, tomato, green beans, kidney beans, and onion in 2½-quart glass salad bowl. Spread Garlic Dressing over top and sprinkle with parsley. Refrigerate, loosely covered, up to 24 hours.

Before serving, toss salad and garnish with egg wedges.

Garlic Dressing

(MAKES ABOUT 1½ CUPS)

- ¾ cup mayonnaise
- ¾ cup sour cream
- 4 cloves garlic, minced
- 1 teaspoon dried basil leaves
- 1 teaspoon dried oregano leaves
- ¾ teaspoon dried tarragon leaves

Combine all ingredients.

PER SERVING

Net Carbohydrate (gm): 15.0   Saturated Fat (gm): 13.3   Protein (gm): 17.7
Calories: 508.1   Cholesterol (mg): 156.8   Carbohydrate (gm): 23.6
Fat (gm): 39.3   Sodium (mg): 659

38 • LOW-CARB VEGETARIAN COOKING

Wilted Spinach Salad

L-O   *An old favorite, updated and streamlined for easy preparation.*

4 SERVINGS (ABOUT 1 CUP EACH)

12 soy bacon slices, cooked and divided
 4 hard-cooked eggs
 8 cups torn spinach leaves
 4 green onions and tops, sliced
²/₃ cup French salad dressing
   Salt and pepper, to taste
   Feta Toast (see p. 9)

Crumble 8 soy bacon slices. Chop 1 hard-cooked egg; cut remaining eggs into quarters. Combine spinach, green onions, crumbled soy bacon and chopped egg in salad bowl. Heat French dressing to boiling in small saucepan; pour over salad and toss. Season to taste with salt and pepper.

Spoon salad onto plates; garnish with egg quarters and remaining soy bacon slices. Serve with Feta Toast.

PER SERVING

Net Carbohydrate (gm): 19.5	Saturated Fat (gm): 8.8	Protein (gm): 21.7
Calories: 528.7	Cholesterol (mg): 236.4	Carbohydrate (gm): 25.7
Fat (gm): 38.8	Sodium (mg): 1333	

Brussels Sprouts and Pasta Shell Salad

L-0 *Make this colorful salad to celebrate the first summer harvest of Brussels sprouts.*

4 SERVINGS (ABOUT 1½ CUPS EACH)

   6 ounces low-carb whole wheat pasta shells, cooked, room temperature
   8 ounces Brussels sprouts, cut into halves, steamed, cooled
   1 cup seeded, chopped tomato
   1 cup sliced purple or green bell pepper
   ¼ cup thinly sliced red onion
      Sun-Dried Tomato and Goat Cheese Dressing (recipe follows)
   ¼ cup (1 ounce) shredded Romano cheese

Combine pasta and vegetables in salad bowl. Pour Sun-Dried Tomato and Goat Cheese Dressing over and toss; sprinkle with cheese.

Sun-Dried Tomato and Goat Cheese Dressing

MAKES ABOUT ½ CUP

- 3 sun-dried tomatoes halves (not in oil), softened, finely chopped
- 2 tablespoons olive oil
- 2 tablespoons white wine vinegar
- 2 tablespoons lemon juice
- 2–3 tablespoons goat cheese
- 2 cloves garlic, minced
- ½ teaspoon dried marjoram leaves
- ¼ teaspoon salt
- ⅛ teaspoon dried thyme leaves
- ⅛ teaspoon pepper

Mix all ingredients.

PER SERVING
Net Carbohydrate (gm): 22.2   Saturated Fat (gm): 2.5   Protein (gm): 17.8
Calories: 297.5   Cholesterol (mg): 8.2   Carbohydrate (gm): 35.1
Fat (gm): 10.2   Sodium (mg): 424

Mixed Vegetable and Macaroni Salad

o	*Substitute other pasta shapes, such as ziti, if you prefer.*

6 SERVINGS (ABOUT 1⅓ CUPS EACH)

- 2 cups thinly sliced zucchini
- 2 cups cut asparagus spears (1½-inch pieces), cooked until crisp-tender
- 1 cup halved cherry tomatoes
- 1 cup sliced carrots, cooked until crisp-tender
- ½ cup frozen peas, thawed
- 8 ounces low-carb whole wheat macaroni, cooked, room temperature
  - Mustard-Turmeric Vinaigrette (recipe follows)
  - Salt and pepper, to taste
- 6 hard-cooked eggs, cut into wedges

Combine vegetables and macaroni in salad bowl; pour Mustard-Turmeric Vinaigrette over and toss. Season to taste with salt and pepper; garnish with egg wedges.

Mustard-Turmeric Vinaigrette

MAKES ABOUT ¾ CUP

- ⅓ cup red wine vinegar
- 3 tablespoons olive oil
- 2–3 tablespoons lemon juice
- 2–3 teaspoons Dijon mustard
- 2 cloves garlic, minced
- ¾ teaspoon ground turmeric

Mix all ingredients.

....

PER SERVING

Net Carbohydrate (gm): 19.2	Saturated Fat (gm): 2.6	Protein (gm): 19.8
Calories: 316.6	Cholesterol (mg): 212.0	Carbohydrate (gm): 30.4
Fat (gm): 13.0	Sodium (mg): 252	

Garden Vegetable and Pasta Salad

L-O *Cook broccoli and cauliflower florets until just crisp-tender for this delicious, meatless entrée.*

4 SERVINGS

- 1 medium eggplant (about 1 pound), unpeeled, cut into $^3/_4$-inch pieces
- 2 tablespoons olive oil
- 2 cups cauliflower florets, cooked, cooled
- 2 cups broccoli florets, cooked, cooled
- 1 cup halved cherry tomatoes
- 1 cup sliced green bell pepper
- 6 ounces low-carb whole wheat fettuccine or linguine, cooked, warm

  Basil Vinaigrette (recipe follows)
- 1 cup (4 ounces) crumbled feta cheese

Line jelly roll pan with aluminum foil and grease lightly. Toss eggplant with oil; arrange on pan and bake at 400 degrees until eggplant is tender, 20 to 30 minutes. Cool.

Combine eggplant, remaining vegetables, and fettuccine in large bowl; pour Basil Vinaigrette over and toss. Spoon onto plates and sprinkle with cheese.

Basil Vinaigrette

MAKES ABOUT ½ CUP

- ¼ cup balsamic vinegar
- 2–3 tablespoons olive oil
- ¼ cup finely chopped fresh or 2 teaspoons dried, basil leaves
- ¼ teaspoon salt
- ¼ teaspoon pepper

Mix all ingredients.

PER SERVING

Net Carbohydrate (gm): 26.3	Saturated Fat (gm): 6.4	Protein (gm): 21.3
Calories: 438.3	Cholesterol (mg): 20.0	Carbohydrate (gm): 43.5
Fat (gm): 21.9	Sodium (mg): 699	

Light Summer Pasta Salad

L-O *The fragrant aroma and flavor of fresh herbs and garlic accent summer-ripe tomatoes in this salad.*

6 SERVINGS

- 10 ounces low-carb whole wheat spaghetti, cooked, room temperature
- 1 pound plum tomatoes, seeded, chopped
- 1 1/2 cups (6 ounces) cubed mozzarella cheese (scant 1/2-inch)
- 1/4 cup finely chopped fresh or 1 tablespoon dried, basil leaves
- 1/4 cup sliced green onions and tops
  Garlic Vinaigrette (recipe follows)

Combine all ingredients except Garlic Vinaigrette in salad bowl; pour Garlic Vinaigrette over and toss.

Garlic Vinaigrette

MAKES ABOUT 2/3 CUP

- 1/3 cup red wine vinegar
- 1/4 cup olive oil
- 4 large cloves garlic, minced
- 1/4 teaspoon salt
- 1/8 teaspoon pepper

Mix all ingredients.

....

PER SERVING

Net Carbohydrate (gm): 19.5	Saturated Fat (gm): 4.9	Protein (gm): 20.6
Calories: 350.8	Cholesterol (mg): 22.1	Carbohydrate (gm): 30.8
Fat (gm): 16.3	Sodium (mg): 429	

Pasta Egg Salad

L-O *Low carb pasta is available in many shapes—choose your favorite for this salad.*

6 SERVINGS (ABOUT ¾ CUP EACH)

  4 ounces low-carb whole wheat macaroni, cooked, room temperature
  6 hard-cooked eggs, coarsely chopped
  4 ounces Cheddar cheese, cubed (½-inch)
  ½ cup sliced edamame pods or snow peas
  ½ cup seeded, chopped tomato
  ¼ cup finely chopped onion
  ¼ cup chopped red bell pepper
    Mayonnaise Dressing (recipe follows)
    Salt and pepper, to taste
 12 lettuce leaves

Combine pasta, eggs, cheese, edamame, tomato, onion, and bell pepper in large bowl; spoon Mayonnaise Dressing over and toss. Season to taste with salt and pepper. Serve salad on lettuce-lined plates.

Mayonnaise Dressing

MAKES ABOUT ⅔ CUP

  ½ cup mayonnaise
  3 tablespoons white wine vinegar
  1 tablespoon Dijon mustard
  ¼ cup finely chopped parsley
  ¼ cup finely chopped chives
  2 tablespoons finely chopped lovage or celery leaves

Mix all ingredients.

....

PER SERVING

Net Carbohydrate (gm): 10.3   Saturated Fat (gm): 7.8   Protein (gm): 18.5
Calories: 381.7   Cholesterol (mg): 238.3   Carbohydrate (gm): 15.6
Fat (gm): 26.6   Sodium (mg): 416.6

Three-Bean, Corn, and Cheese Salad

L | *This salad travels well for picnics or shared dinners; make up to 2 days in advance and refrigerate, adding cheese just before serving.*

6 SERVINGS (ABOUT 1 CUP EACH)

12 ounces cut green beans, steamed, cooled
 1 can (15 ounces) garbanzo beans, rinsed, drained
 1 can (15 ounces) kidney beans, rinsed, drained
 $^1/_2$ cup frozen whole kernel corn, thawed
 $^1/_2$ cup chopped red bell pepper
 $^1/_2$ cup sliced green onions and tops
 6 ounces brick or mozzarella cheese, cubed ($^1/_2$-inch)
 $^2/_3$ cup French salad dressing
12 lettuce leaves

Combine vegetables and cheese in salad bowl; drizzle with dressing and toss. Serve on lettuce-lined plates.

PER SERVING
Net Carbohydrate (gm): 30.0   Saturated Fat (gm): 7.0   Protein (gm): 15.8
Calories: 411.8   Cholesterol (mg): 26.3   Carbohydrate (gm): 40.6
Fat (gm): 22.0   Sodium (mg): 848

El Paso Bean and Corn Salad

[L-O] *For variation, roll salad mixture in warm low-carb whole wheat tortillas instead of serving with Garlic Bread.*

8 SERVINGS (ABOUT ⅔ CUP EACH)

- 2 cans (15 ounces each) pinto beans, rinsed, drained
- 1 can (15 ounces) black beans, rinsed, drained
- ½ cup frozen thawed whole kernel corn
- ⅓ cup sliced green onions and tops
- 1½ cups (6 ounces) shredded Mexican cheese blend, divided
- ½ cup garlic ranch dressing
- 5 cups salad greens
- Garlic Bread (recipe follows)

Combine beans, corn, green onions, and ³/₄ cup cheese in salad bowl; add garlic ranch dressing and toss. Spoon salad onto salad greens on plates; sprinkle with remaining ³/₄ cup cheese. Serve with Garlic Bread.

Garlic Bread

MAKES 8 PIECES

- 8 slices low-carb whole wheat bread
- 3 tablespoons butter, softened
- 1 small clove garlic, minced

Spread bread slices with combined butter and garlic. Broil 6 inches from heat source until toasted, 2 to 3 minutes.

PER SERVING

Net Carbohydrate (gm): 26.6	Saturated Fat (gm): 8.2	Protein (gm): 17.0
Calories: 407.6	Cholesterol (mg): 33.3	Carbohydrate (gm): 37.8
Fat (gm): 21.7	Sodium (mg): 919	

Mixed Bean and Cheese Salad with Ginger Dressing

L | *This recipe can easily be doubled or tripled for potluck gatherings.*

8 SERVINGS (ABOUT ¾ CUP EACH)

12 ounces cut green beans, cooked until crisp-tender
1 can (15 ounces) pinto beans, rinsed, drained
1 can (15 ounces) black beans, rinsed, drained
½ can (15 ounce-size) dark red kidney beans, rinsed, drained
8 ounces brick cheese, cubed
¼ cup sliced green onions and tops
    Ginger Dressing (recipe follows)
    Salt and pepper, to taste
16 medium iceberg lettuce leaves

Combine beans, cheese, and green onions in large bowl; pour Ginger Dressing over and toss. Season to taste with salt and pepper. Serve on lettuce-lined plates.

Ginger Dressing

MAKES ABOUT ¾ CUP

¼ cup canola oil
⅓ cup sugar-free pineapple or apricot preserves
3 tablespoons cider or rice wine vinegar
2 tablespoons packed light brown sugar
1 teaspoon minced gingerroot

Mix all ingredients.

....

PER SERVING

Net Carbohydrate (gm): 23.3   Saturated Fat (gm): 5.9   Protein (gm): 14.0
Calories: 310.5   Cholesterol (mg): 26.3   Carbohydrate (gm): 31.2
Fat (gm): 15.7   Sodium (mg): 577

Mediterranean Salad

L Garbanzo beans are authentic to Mediterranean recipes; kidney, black, and pinto beans have about one-third less carbs, if you care to substitute.

6 SERVINGS (ABOUT 1 CUP EACH)

1 can (15 ounces) garbanzo beans, rinsed, drained
1 1/2 cups seeded, chopped tomatoes
1 1/2 cups cubed zucchini
1 1/2 cups chopped parsley
1 cup chopped green bell pepper
1/4 cup sliced green onions and tops
1/4 cup pine nuts, toasted
1/4 cup olive oil
1/4 cup lemon juice
3 cloves garlic, minced
Salt and pepper, to taste
6 slices Feta Toast (see p. 9)

Combine beans, tomatoes, zucchini, parsley, bell pepper, green onions, and pine nuts in salad bowl. Combine olive oil, lemon juice, and garlic; drizzle over salad and toss. Season to taste with salt and pepper. Serve with Feta Toast.

....

PER SERVING

Net Carbohydrate (gm): 28.6	Saturated Fat (gm): 5.8	Protein (gm): 15.9
Calories: 396.8	Cholesterol (mg): 24.9	Carbohydrate (gm): 38.4
Fat (gm): 22.3	Sodium (mg): 735	

Greek Islands Salad

Flavors of the Mediterranean will enhance any meal!

6 SERVINGS (ABOUT 1 CUP EACH)

    6 cups torn romaine lettuce leaves

    1 can (15 ounces) garbanzo beans, rinsed, drained

1 1/2 cups tomato wedges

    6 hard-cooked eggs, cut into wedges or sliced

    1 cup sliced, peeled cucumber

    1 cup quartered artichoke hearts

    1 cup thinly sliced green, yellow, and red bell peppers

   12 Greek olives

 1/4 cup thinly sliced red onion

    1 cup (4 ounces) crumbled feta cheese

 3/4 cup garlic vinaigrette

     Oregano sprigs, as garnish

Arrange lettuce leaves on salad plates; arrange remaining ingredients, except feta cheese, garlic vinaigrette, and oregano sprigs, on lettuce. Sprinkle salads with feta cheese, drizzle with vinaigrette, and garnish with oregano sprigs.

. . . .

PER SERVING

Net Carbohydrate (gm): 21.3	Saturated Fat (gm): 7.6	Protein (gm): 15.8
Calories: 389	Cholesterol (mg): 234.0	Carbohydrate (gm): 28.2
Fat (gm): 24.0	Sodium (mg): 957	

Lentil Salad with Feta Cheese

L | *Cook the lentils just until tender so they retain their shape.*

6 SERVINGS (ABOUT 1⅓ CUPS EACH)

1¼ cups dried brown lentils
2½ cups canned vegetable broth
1½ cups coarsely chopped iceberg lettuce
1½ cups chopped tomatoes
½ cup thinly sliced celery
½ cup sliced yellow bell pepper
½ cup chopped, seeded cucumber
½ cup chopped onion
¾ cup (3 ounces) crumbled feta cheese
Balsamic Dressing (recipe follows)
Salt and pepper, to taste
Lettuce leaves, as garnish

Wash and sort lentils, discarding any stones. Heat lentils and broth to boiling in large saucepan; reduce heat and simmer, covered, until lentils are just tender, about 25 minutes. Drain any excess liquid; cool to room temperature.

Combine lentils, lettuce, vegetables, and cheese in salad bowl; drizzle Balsamic Dressing over and toss. Season to taste with salt and pepper. Serve on lettuce-lined plates.

Balsamic Dressing

MAKES ABOUT ⅓ CUP

3 tablespoons balsamic or red wine vinegar

2 tablespoons olive oil

2 tablespoons lemon juice

2 cloves garlic, minced

$^1/_2$ teaspoon dried thyme leaves

Mix all ingredients.

PER SERVING

Net Carbohydrate (gm): 18.5   Saturated Fat (gm): 2.6   Protein (gm): 14.7
Calories: 252.5   Cholesterol (mg): 8.3   Carbohydrate (gm): 32.6
Fat (gm): 8.2   Sodium (mg): 367

Quinoa Tabbouleh

L *Two healthy grains, bulgur and quinoa, combine in this tasty version of tabbouleh.*

4 SERVINGS (ABOUT 1¼ CUPS EACH)

$\frac{1}{2}$ cup bulgur (cracked wheat)

$\frac{1}{3}$ cup quinoa, cooked, cooled

1 cup quartered cherry tomatoes

$\frac{3}{4}$ cup thinly sliced green onions and tops

$\frac{3}{4}$ cup finely chopped fresh parsley

$\frac{1}{4}$ cup finely chopped fresh mint

1 cup (4 ounces) cubed or coarsely crumbled, feta cheese

1 cup plain yogurt

$\frac{1}{2}$ cup toasted pine nuts or almonds

$\frac{1}{4}$–$\frac{1}{3}$ cup lemon juice

1$\frac{1}{2}$–2 tablespoons olive oil

Salt and pepper, to taste

Pour boiling water over bulgur to cover; let stand 15 minutes or until bulgur is tender but slightly chewy. Drain well.

Mix bulgur, quinoa, tomatoes, green onions, parsley, and mint; stir in feta cheese, yogurt, pine nuts, lemon juice, and oil. Season to taste with salt and pepper. Refrigerate 1 to 2 hours for flavors to blend.

PER SERVING

Net Carbohydrate (gm): 30	Saturated Fat (gm): 7.7	Protein (gm): 14.3
Calories: 436	Cholesterol (mg): 27.5	Carbohydrate (gm): 37.2
Fat (gm): 27.5	Sodium (mg): 371	

Wheat Berry, Quinoa, and Vegetable Salad

L *Wheat berries and quinoa combine for great flavor and texture in this healthful salad.*

6 SERVINGS (ABOUT 1 CUP EACH)

  1 cup cooked wheat berries, room temperature
  1 cup cooked quinoa, room temperature
  1 1/2 cups coarsely chopped ripe tomatoes
  1 1/2 cups cubed zucchini
  1 1/2 cups cubed, seeded cucumbers
  1/2 cup sliced green onions and tops
  1/4 cup finely chopped parsley
    Roasted Garlic Vinaigrette (recipe follows)
    Salt and pepper, to taste
  3 cups cottage cheese
    Curly endive or escarole

Combine wheat berries, quinoa, vegetables, and parsley in salad bowl; pour Roasted Garlic Vinaigrette over and toss. Season to taste with salt and pepper. Spoon salad and cottage cheese onto endive-lined plates.

Roasted Garlic Vinaigrette

MAKES ABOUT 1/2 CUP

  1/4 cup olive oil
  1/4 cup balsamic vinegar
  2–3 teaspoons minced roasted garlic
  1 teaspoon dried oregano leaves

Mix all ingredients.

....

PER SERVING

Net Carbohydrate (gm): 24.6	Saturated Fat (gm): 4.3	Protein (gm): 17.9
Calories: 310.0	Cholesterol (mg): 15.8	Carbohydrate (gm): 26.6
Fat (gm): 15.5	Sodium (mg): 436	

Roasted Vegetable and Wild Rice Salad with Warm Goat Cheese

| L | *Brown rice or another grain can be substituted for the wild rice, if desired.* |

8 SERVINGS (ABOUT 1 CUP EACH)

   1 cup sliced yellow summer squash
   1 cup sliced zucchini
   1 pound eggplant, peeled, cut into 1-inch pieces
   1 cup red bell pepper pieces ($1^{1}/_{2}$-inch)
   4 large cloves garlic, peeled
   1 tablespoon olive oil
   1 tablespoon herbes de Provence
$1^{1}/_{2}$ cups cooked wild rice, room temperature
   $^{2}/_{3}$ cup Balsamic Dressing (see p. 53)
     Salt and pepper, to taste
 10 ounces goat cheese, cut into 4 pieces
   2 tablespoons butter, softened
   4 slices low-carb whole wheat bread, toasted

Line jelly roll pan with aluminum foil and grease lightly. Arrange vegetables in single layer on pan; drizzle with oil and sprinkle with herbs. Roast vegetables at 425 degrees until browned and tender, about 40 minutes, removing garlic when soft, after about 20 minutes; reserve garlic. Cool vegetables to room temperature.

Combine vegetables and rice in serving bowl; drizzle Balsamic Dressing over and toss. Season to taste with salt and pepper. Arrange salad on plates.

Bake cheese in greased baking pan at 350 degrees until warm, 5 to 8 minutes; arrange on tops of salads. Mash reserved garlic cloves and mix with butter; spread on toast and serve with the salads.

....

PER SERVING

Net Carbohydrate (gm): 24.1   Saturated Fat (gm): 6.9   Protein (gm): 13.1
Calories: 333.3   Cholesterol (mg): 21.1   Carbohydrate (gm): 31.0
Fat (gm): 19.4   Sodium (mg): 382

CHAPTER THREE

Breakfast
&
Brunch

Honey-Walnut Yogurt

| L | *A nutritious breakfast that's also quick and easy.*

2 SERVINGS

> 2 cups plain yogurt
> $^1/_4$–$^1/_2$ cup walnut pieces, toasted
> 2–4 teaspoons honey

Spoon yogurt into bowls; sprinkle with walnuts and drizzle with honey.

PER SERVING

Net Carbohydrate (gm): 25.7	Saturated Fat (gm): 10.1	Protein (gm): 14.3
Calories: 468.7	Cholesterol (mg): 43.5	Carbohydrate (gm): 27.8
Fat (gm): 33.7	Sodium (mg): 138	

Best Breakfast Oatmeal

L *Oatmeal so delicious it can be served as company fare!*

4 SERVINGS

- 3 cups water
- 1 1/2 cups quick-cooking oats
- 2/3 cup toasted slivered almonds
- 1/4 cup ground flax seeds
- 1/4 cup dried cranberries or dried fruit bits
- Ground cinnamon
- 1/4 cup sugar-free pancake syrup
- 1/2 cup light cream
- 8 soy bacon slices, cooked

Heat water to boiling in large saucepan; stir in oats. Reduce heat and simmer, stirring occasionally, until thickened, 2 to 3 minutes; stir in almonds and flax seeds.

Sprinkle each serving with cranberries and cinnamon and drizzle with syrup and cream. Serve with soy bacon slices.

PER SERVING

Net Carbohydrate (gm): 28.8	Saturated Fat (gm): 5.7	Protein (gm): 12.6
Calories: 416	Cholesterol (mg): 19.8	Carbohydrate (gm): 38.4
Fat (gm): 25.7	Sodium (mg): 184	

Buckwheat Pancakes, Sausage 'n Eggs

L-O   *Cook the eggs sunny-side-up or over easy!*

6 SERVINGS

- 1 cup reduced-fat buttermilk
- 1 egg
- 1 tablespoon canola oil
- 1/2 cup whole wheat pastry flour
- 1/3 cup buckwheat flour
- 1 tablespoon packed light brown sugar
- 1 teaspoon baking powder
- 1/2 teaspoon baking soda
- 1/2 teaspoon salt
- 1 teaspoon grated orange rind
- 1/2-1 cup sugar-free pancake syrup
- 6 fried eggs
- 12 soy sausage patties (about 18 ounces), cooked

Mix buttermilk, egg, and oil in medium bowl. Add combined remaining ingredients, except pancake syrup, eggs, and sausage patties; beat until almost smooth.

Pour batter into lightly greased large skillet, using about 1/4 cup batter for each pancake. Cook over medium heat until bubbles form in pancakes and they are browned on the bottoms, 3 to 5 minutes. Turn pancakes; cook until browned on other side, 3 to 5 minutes.

Serve pancakes with syrup, eggs, and sausage.

....

PER SERVING

Net Carbohydrate (gm): 24.4   Saturated Fat (gm): 4.9   Protein (gm): 25.4
Calories: 419   Cholesterol (mg): 247.1   Carbohydrate (gm): 28.8
Fat (gm): 24.8   Sodium (mg): 1233

Vegetable Hash and Eggs

L-0 *Fry or poach the eggs, as you prefer, and serve them alongside the hash.*

4 SERVINGS

1 cup chopped red or green bell pepper

$1/4$ cup chopped green onions and tops

1–2 tablespoons olive or canola oil

2 cups cubed, cooked unpeeled Idaho potatoes

1 cup cubed zucchini

$3/4$ cup halved cherry tomatoes

$1/2$–1 teaspoon dried thyme leaves

Salt and pepper, to taste

8 eggs

4 slices low-carb whole wheat bread, toasted

4 teaspoons butter

Sauté bell pepper and green onions in oil in large skillet 3 to 4 minutes; add potatoes and zucchini and cook over medium heat until potatoes are browned and zucchini is tender, stirring frequently, about 5 minutes. Add tomatoes and thyme; cook 2 to 3 minutes longer. Season to taste with salt and pepper.

Move hash to side of skillet; add eggs to center of skillet. Cook, covered, over low heat until eggs are cooked, 3 to 4 minutes; season to taste with salt and pepper. Spread toast with butter and serve with hash.

PER SERVING

Net Carbohydrate (gm): 24.5	Saturated Fat (gm): 5.7	Protein (gm): 19.1
Calories: 362.6	Cholesterol (mg): 433.8	Carbohydrate (gm): 30.5
Fat (gm): 19.2	Sodium (mg): 310	

Sweet Potato Hash with Poached Eggs

L-O *Serve this sweet hash with crisp soy bacon strips, if you like. They are available in both the refrigerated and frozen section of the grocery store.*

4 SERVINGS

$1/2$ cup chopped red bell pepper

$1/4$ cup sliced green onions and tops

1–2 tablespoons canola oil

2 cups cubed, cooked sweet potatoes

1 teaspoon dried rosemary leaves

$1/2$ teaspoon dried thyme leaves

Salt and pepper, to taste

8 poached or fried eggs

4 slices low-carb whole wheat bread, toasted

4 teaspoons butter

Sauté bell pepper and green onions in oil in large skillet 2 to 3 minutes. Add sweet potatoes and herbs; cook, uncovered, over medium heat until vegetables are lightly browned and tender, about 10 minutes. Season to taste with salt and pepper. Spoon hash onto plates and top with eggs. Spread toast with butter.

PER SERVING

Net Carbohydrate (gm): 17.6
Calories: 331.7
Fat (gm): 19

Saturated Fat (gm): 5.4
Cholesterol (mg): 432.8
Sodium (mg): 463

Protein (gm): 17.9
Carbohydrate (gm): 23.3

Hash Brown Loaf with Eggs

L-O

Serve this tasty loaf with soy bacon slices, if you like. For flavor variation, use shredded Gruyere, mozzarella, or Pepper-Jack cheese instead of the Cheddar.

4 SERVINGS

$3/4$ cup textured vegetable protein

$3/4$ cup vegetable broth

1 cup shredded carrots

1 small onion, finely chopped

$1/4$ cup chopped red bell pepper

2 cloves garlic, minced

1 tablespoon canola oil

$3/4$ cup shredded Idaho potatoes

$1 1/2$ teaspoons dried thyme leaves

1 teaspoon snipped chives

Salt and pepper, to taste

4 eggs, lightly beaten

1 cup (4 ounces) Cheddar cheese, divided

Combine vegetable protein and broth in medium bowl; let stand until broth is absorbed, 5 to 10 minutes.

Sauté carrots, onion, bell pepper, and garlic in oil in large skillet until tender, about 5 minutes. Stir in potatoes and herbs; season to taste with salt and pepper. Mix in eggs and $3/4$ cup cheese.

Pack mixture into greased $7 1/2$ x $3 3/4$-inch loaf pan. Bake, loosely covered, at 350 degrees 45 minutes; uncover and sprinkle with remaining $1/4$ cup cheese. Bake until loaf is set and cheese melted, about 15 minutes longer. Let stand 10 minutes before serving.

Loosen sides of loaf with sharp knife; unmold onto serving plate and cut into slices.

....

PER SERVING

Net Carbohydrate (gm): 14.2	Saturated Fat (gm): 7.8	Protein (gm): 23.8
Calories: 337.1	Cholesterol (mg): 241.2	Carbohydrate (gm): 19.6
Fat (gm): 18.4	Sodium (mg): 639	

Breakfast Pizza

Great for breakfast, brunch, or a light supper. The eggs are added last and quickly cooked in the oven.

6 SERVINGS

Whole Wheat Pizza Dough (recipe follows)
1 cup pizza sauce
4 ounces soy sausage patties, crumbled
$1/2$ cup sliced green bell pepper
$1/4$ cup thinly sliced onion
$1^1/_2$ cups (6 ounces) mozzarella cheese
2 eggs

Spread Whole Wheat Pizza Dough on lightly greased 12-inch pizza pan, making rim around edge; spread evenly with pizza sauce. Sprinkle pizza with soy sausage, green pepper, onion, and cheese. Bake at 425 degrees until pizza is lightly browned, 15 to 20 minutes.

Remove pizza from oven. Break eggs into center of pizza; stir with a fork and quickly spread over pizza; return to oven and bake until eggs are cooked, 2 to 3 minutes.

Whole Wheat Pizza Dough

MAKES ONE 12-INCH CRUST

    1 cup whole wheat pastry flour, divided

    1 package fast-rising yeast

    $1/4$ teaspoon salt

    $1/2$ cup very hot water (120 degrees)

    2 teaspoons honey

Combine $3/4$ cup flour, yeast, and salt in medium bowl; add hot water and honey, stirring until smooth. Mix in enough remaining flour to make a soft dough. Knead dough on floured surface until smooth and elastic, about 5 minutes. Cover and let stand 15 minutes before using.

....

PER SERVING

Net Carbohydrate (gm): 20.4   Saturated Fat (gm): 3.4   Protein (gm): 15.8

Calories: 233.8   Cholesterol (mg): 88.4   Carbohydrate (gm): 24.9

Fat (gm): 8.2   Sodium (mg): 786

Eggs with Welsh Rarebit

L-O *The distinctively flavored cheese sauce is rich and delicious.
The bread can be toasted instead of pan-grilled, if desired.*

6 SERVINGS (ABOUT ½ CUP SAUCE EACH)

1/4 cup very finely chopped onion

3 tablespoons butter

1/4 cup all-purpose flour

2 cups reduced-fat milk

1/2 cup white wine

2 ounces pasteurized processed cheese, cubed

1/2 cup (2 ounces) shredded sharp Cheddar cheese

1/4–1/2 teaspoon dry mustard

1/2 teaspoon Worcestershire sauce

White and cayenne pepper, to taste

6 slices low-carb whole wheat bread

Vegetable cooking spray

6 thick slices tomato

6 fried or poached eggs

Chopped parsley leaves, as garnish

Sauté onion in butter in medium saucepan until tender, 2 to 3 minutes.
Stir in flour and cook over medium-low heat, stirring constantly, 1 minute.
Whisk in milk and wine; heat to boiling. Boil, whisking constantly, until
thickened, about 1 minute.

Stir in cheeses, dry mustard, and Worcestershire sauce; reduce heat to
low and cook until cheeses are melted. Season to taste with white and
cayenne pepper.

Spray both sides of bread with cooking spray; cook over medium heat
in large skillet until browned, 2 to 3 minutes on each side. Broil tomato
slices 4 inches from heat source until hot through. Arrange bread on
plates; top with tomato slices and eggs. Spoon cheese sauce over and
sprinkle with parsley.

PER SERVING

Net Carbohydrate (gm): 15.7   Saturated Fat (gm): 9.3   Protein (gm): 18.3
Calories: 341.0   Cholesterol (mg): 253.0   Carbohydrate (gm): 19.2
Fat (gm): 20.4   Sodium (mg): 405

Eggs Napoleon

L-O *You'll enjoy this new twist on the old favorite, Eggs Benedict.*

6 SERVINGS

  6 slices low-carb whole wheat bread, toasted
    Spinach leaves, as garnish
 12 soy bacon slices, cooked
  6 slices tomato
  6 poached eggs
    Cream Cheese Hollandaise (recipe follows)
    Paprika, as garnish
    Chopped parsley, as garnish

Top toast with spinach leaves, soy bacon slices, tomato, and poached eggs. Spoon Cream Cheese Hollandaise over eggs; sprinkle with paprika and parsley.

Cream Cheese Hollandaise

MAKES ABOUT 1½ CUPS

    2 packages (3 ounces each) cream cheese, softened
  ⅓ cup sour cream
 3–4 tablespoons reduced-fat milk
 1–2 teaspoons lemon juice
½–1 teaspoon Dijon mustard
  ½ teaspoon ground turmeric

Heat all ingredients in small saucepan over medium-low to low heat until melted and smooth, stirring constantly.

....

PER SERVING

Net Carbohydrate (gm): 8.8	Saturated Fat (gm): 9.7	Protein (gm): 14.2
Calories: 293.8	Cholesterol (mg): 247.5	Carbohydrate (gm): 12.3
Fat (gm): 21.7	Sodium (mg): 527	

Eggs Peperonata

L-O   *Peperonata lends Italian flavor to this popular egg dish.*

4 SERVINGS

Peperonata (recipe follows)
1 cup chopped tomato
6 eggs
2 tablespoons reduced-fat milk
$^{1}/_{2}$ cup (2 ounces) shredded Cheddar cheese
Salt and pepper, to taste

Make Peperonata, adding chopped tomato during last 10 minutes of cooking time.

Beat eggs and milk. Move Peperonata to side of skillet and add eggs to center. Cook until eggs are set, stirring occasionally; sprinkle with cheese. Gently stir egg mixture into Peperonata; season to taste with salt and pepper.

Peperonata

MAKES ABOUT 1½ CUPS

    2 cups sliced red and green bell peppers
    1 cup sliced onion
  4–6 cloves garlic, minced
  1–2 tablespoons olive oil
  ¼ cup water
  ¾ teaspoon Italian seasoning
    Salt and pepper, to taste

Cook bell peppers, onion, and garlic in oil in large skillet over medium heat 5 minutes. Add water and Italian seasoning; cook, covered, over medium-low to low heat until vegetables are very tender and creamy, 20 to 25 minutes, stirring occasionally. Season to taste with salt and pepper.

PER SERVING

Net Carbohydrate (gm): 9.4	Saturated Fat (gm): 5.8	Protein (gm): 14.9
Calories: 246.1	Cholesterol (mg): 332.2	Carbohydrate (gm): 11.9
Fat (gm): 15.8	Sodium (mg): 202	

Quiche Lorraine

A high-carb pastry crust is replaced with a low-carb coating of bread crumbs in this great quiche recipe.

6 SERVINGS

2–3 tablespoons unseasoned dry bread crumbs

$^1/_4$ cup finely chopped onion

1 tablespoon butter

$^3/_4$ cup reduced-fat milk

$^1/_2$ can (12-ounce size) evaporated milk

3 eggs

$^1/_4$ cup sour cream

$^1/_4$ teaspoon salt

$^1/_8$ teaspoon cayenne pepper

$^1/_8$ teaspoon ground nutmeg

$1^1/_4$ cups (5 ounces) shredded Swiss cheese

1 tablespoon all-purpose flour

18 soy bacon slices, cooked

Sprinkle lightly greased 8- or 9-inch pie pan with bread crumbs.

Sauté onion in butter in small skillet until tender, 3 to 5 minutes. Mix milks, eggs, sour cream, salt, cayenne, and nutmeg in medium bowl until smooth. Toss cheese with flour; stir into milk mixture. Stir in onion. Pour into prepared pie pan and bake at 350 degrees until set in the center, and a sharp knife inserted near center comes out clean, about 40 minutes. Cool quiche on wire rack 5 minutes before cutting. Serve with soy bacon slices.

Spinach Quiche—Drain $1/2$ package (10-ounce size) frozen, thawed spinach between paper toweling. Prepare recipe as directed, adding spinach to onion in skillet and cooking over medium to medium-low heat until mixture is quite dry, 3 to 4 minutes. Proceed as directed.

Quiche El Rancho—Substitute Monterey Jack cheese for the Swiss; sprinkle each serving with chopped cilantro. Substitute "Chorizo" (see p. 81), for the bacon, forming the "Chorizo" into patties and browning in a greased skillet.

PER SERVING

Net Carbohydrate (gm): 9.2	Saturated Fat (gm): 9.1	Protein (gm): 15.3
Calories: 284.2	Cholesterol (mg): 147.1	Carbohydrate (gm): 9.8
Fat (gm): 20.4	Sodium (mg): 484	

Omelet Puff with Vegetable Mélange

L-O *To save morning preparation time, make the Vegetable Mélange a day in advance and reheat at serving time.*

2 SERVINGS

> 4 egg whites
> 2 whole eggs
> $1/4$ teaspoon dried tarragon leaves
> $1/4$ teaspoon salt
> $1/4$ teaspoon pepper
> $1/4$ cup (1 ounce) shredded brick cheese
> Vegetable Mélange (recipe follows)

Beat egg whites in large bowl until foamy; beat at high speed until stiff, but not dry, peaks form. Beat whole eggs, tarragon, salt, and pepper at high speed in small bowl until thick and lemon-colored. Fold egg white mixture into egg mixture; fold in cheese.

Cook egg mixture in greased oven-proof skillet over medium to medium-low heat until bottom of omelet is light brown, about 5 minutes. Transfer to oven and bake at 325 degrees, uncovered, until omelet is puffed and light brown, 15 to 20 minutes. Loosen edge of omelet with spatula; slide onto serving platter, carefully folding omelet in half. Spoon Vegetable Mélange over omelet.

Vegetable Mélange

MAKES ABOUT 1½ CUPS

    1 cup sliced zucchini
   ⅔ cup sliced green bell pepper
   ⅓ cup sliced onion
    1 medium tomato, cut into wedges
1–2 tablespoons olive oil
1–2 tablespoons water
     Salt and pepper, to taste

Sauté vegetables in oil in medium skillet 3 to 5 minutes. Add water; cook, covered, over medium-low heat until tender, about 5 minutes. Season to taste with salt and pepper.

PER SERVING

Net Carbohydrate (gm): 4.8   Saturated Fat (gm): 4.5   Protein (gm): 17.8
Calories: 211.9   Cholesterol (mg): 224.7   Carbohydrate (gm): 6.2
Fat (gm): 12.8   Sodium (mg): 555

Cheddar Cheese Soufflé

L-O *Chili Tomato Sauce (see p. 83) can be served as a delicious accompaniment to the soufflé.*

4 SERVINGS

1–2 tablespoons grated Parmesan cheese

1 cup reduced-fat milk

3 tablespoons all-purpose flour

1 tablespoon chopped chives

$^1/_2$ teaspoon dried marjoram leaves

$^1/_2$ teaspoon dry mustard

$^1/_4$ teaspoon cayenne pepper

1–2 pinches ground nutmeg

3 egg yolks

1 cup (4 ounces) shredded Cheddar cheese

Salt and white pepper, to taste

3 egg whites

$^1/_4$ teaspoon cream of tartar

Attach an aluminum foil collar to 1-quart soufflé dish, extending foil 3 inches above top of dish; lightly grease inside of dish and collar and sprinkle with Parmesan cheese.

Mix milk and flour until smooth in small saucepan; mix in chives, marjoram, dry mustard, cayenne, and nutmeg. Heat to boiling, whisking constantly; boil until thickened, about 1 minute, whisking constantly. Whisk about $^1/_2$ cup mixture into egg yolks in small bowl; whisk egg mixture back into saucepan. Add cheese and cook over low heat until melted, whisking constantly. Season to taste with salt and white pepper.

Beat egg whites in medium bowl until foamy; add cream of tartar and beat at high speed until stiff, but not dry, peaks form. Stir $^1/_3$ of the egg whites into cheese mixture; fold cheese mixture into remaining whites in bowl. Spoon into prepared soufflé dish. Bake at 350 degrees until soufflé is puffed, browned, and just set in the center, 35 to 40 minutes. Serve immediately.

PER SERVING

Net Carbohydrate (gm): 8.4	Saturated Fat (gm): 7.9	Protein (gm): 14.9
Calories: 226.9	Cholesterol (mg): 189.2	Carbohydrate (gm): 8.7
Fat (gm): 14.5	Sodium (mg): 271	

Vegetable Frittata with Parmesan Toast

L-O *An Italian-style vegetable omelet that's quick and easy to prepare, delicious to eat!*

4 SERVINGS

    2 cups sliced mushrooms
    1 cup chopped green bell pepper
  $1/4$ cup thinly sliced green onions and tops
    2 cloves garlic, minced
    2 tablespoons olive oil
  $1/4$ cup water
    6 eggs
  $1/4$ cup reduced-fat milk
  $3/4$ cup (3 ounces) shredded Cheddar cheese
  $1/4$ teaspoon salt
  $1/8$ teaspoon pepper
    Parmesan Toast (recipe follows)

Sauté vegetables and garlic in oil in large oven-proof skillet 5 minutes; add water and simmer, covered, over medium heat until vegetables are tender and liquid is absorbed, about 5 minutes.

Beat eggs and milk; mix in cheese, salt, and pepper. Pour mixture over vegetables and cook without stirring, uncovered, over medium-low heat until eggs are set and lightly browned on bottom, about 10 minutes.

Broil frittata 6 inches from heat source until cooked on top, 3 to 4 minutes; invert frittata onto serving plate. Serve with Parmesan Toast.

Parmesan Toast

2 slices low-carb whole wheat bread, cut diagonally into halves

$^{1}/_{4}$ cup (1 ounce) shredded Parmesan cheese

Sprinkle bread slices with Parmesan cheese; broil 6 inches from heat source until browned, 2 to 3 minutes.

....

PER SERVING

Net Carbohydrate (gm): 9.3	Saturated Fat (gm): 8.8	Protein (gm): 21.2
Calories: 341.0	Cholesterol (mg): 345.1	Carbohydrate (gm): 11.5
Fat (gm): 24.0	Sodium (mg): 536	

Polenta Spoon Bread with Poached Eggs and Soy Sausage

L-O *A Southern favorite that will have folks begging for seconds!*

8 SERVINGS

1 medium red bell pepper, chopped
2 tablespoons minced garlic
1 tablespoon olive oil
3 egg yolks
2 1/2 cups reduced-fat milk
1 cup polenta or yellow cornmeal
1 1/2 teaspoons salt
1 teaspoon dried Italian seasoning
1/8–1/4 teaspoon red pepper flakes
2 tablespoons melted butter
1/4 cup (1 ounce) grated Parmesan cheese
3 egg whites, beaten to stiff peaks
8 poached or fried eggs
2 tablespoons snipped fresh chives
8 soy sausage patties (about 12 ounces), cooked

Sauté bell pepper and garlic in oil in small skillet until tender, 2 to 3 minutes. Cool.

Whisk egg yolks and milk until smooth in medium saucepan; heat to boiling, whisking constantly. Whisk in polenta and salt gradually; reduce heat to medium and whisk in bell pepper mixture, Italian seasoning, and pepper flakes. Simmer 2 minutes, stirring constantly with wooden spoon. Remove from heat; stir in butter and cheese.

Fold beaten egg whites into polenta mixture; pour into greased 2-quart soufflé dish or casserole. Bake at 375 degrees until puffed and golden, about 30 minutes. Spoon onto plates; top with eggs and sprinkle with chives. Serve with soy sausage patties.

....

PER SERVING

Net Carbohydrate (gm): 18.9	Saturated Fat (gm): 6.3	Protein (gm): 20.7
Calories: 350.0	Cholesterol (mg): 304.2	Carbohydrate (gm): 21.5
Fat (gm): 21.1	Sodium (mg): 1046	

Pinto Bean Cheesecake with Chili Tomato Sauce

L-O | *Make the cheesecake a day in advance, as overnight chilling is essential. Serve at room temperature, or heated as the recipe directs.*

10 SERVINGS

5 low-carb whole wheat tortillas (6-inch), warmed
3 packages (8 ounces each) cream cheese, softened
6 eggs
1 can (15 ounces) pinto beans, rinsed, drained
1/2 jalapeño chili, finely chopped
2 tablespoons finely chopped onion
2 cloves garlic, minced
2 teaspoons Worcestershire sauce
2 teaspoons ground cumin
1/2 teaspoon dried oregano leaves
1/2 teaspoon chili powder
1/2 teaspoon salt
1/2 teaspoon cayenne pepper
Chili Tomato Sauce (see p. 83)

Lightly grease 9-inch springform pan and line bottom with overlapping tortillas.

Beat cream cheese in large bowl until fluffy; beat in eggs. Mix in remaining ingredients, except Chili-Tomato Sauce, and pour into pan. Bake at 300 degrees until center is set and sharp knife inserted halfway between center and edge of cheesecake comes out almost clean, 1 3/4 to 2 hours. Cool to room temperature on wire rack. Refrigerate overnight.

Cook wedges of cheesecake in greased skillet over medium-low heat until browned on both sides. Serve with Chili Tomato Sauce.

PER SERVING

Net Carbohydrate (gm): 10.3
Calories: 362.5
Fat (gm): 28.7

Saturated Fat (gm): 16.0
Cholesterol (mg): 201.7
Sodium (mg): 583

Protein (gm): 14.1
Carbohydrate (gm): 17.1

Eggs Scrambled with Crisp Tortilla Strips

L-O · *Serve "Chorizo" (see pg. 81) with this dish; shape the mixture into patties and cook until browned in a greased skillet.*

6 SERVINGS

> 3 low-carb whole wheat tortillas (6-inch), cut into 2 x $^1/_2$-inch strips
>
> Vegetable cooking spray
>
> 12 eggs
>
> 3 tablespoons reduced-fat milk
>
> Salt and pepper, to taste
>
> $^1/_2$ cup (2 ounces) crumbled Mexican white cheese or shredded Monterey Jack cheese
>
> 6 tablespoons finely chopped cilantro
>
> $^3/_4$ cup mild or hot salsa

Spray tortilla strips lightly with cooking spray; cook in skillet over medium to medium-high heat until browned and crisp.

Move tortilla strips to side of skillet; beat eggs and milk until foamy and pour next to tortilla strips in skillet. Cook over medium to medium-low heat until eggs are just set, stirring occasionally; gently combine eggs and tortilla strips. Season to taste with salt and pepper; sprinkle with cheese and cilantro. Serve with salsa.

PER SERVING

Net Carbohydrate (gm): 5.1	Saturated Fat (gm): 5.0	Protein (gm): 17.4
Calories: 221.3	Cholesterol (mg): 433.5	Carbohydrate (gm): 9.1
Fat (gm): 13.9	Sodium (mg): 560	

Mexican Scrambled Eggs with "Chorizo"

L-0 *Crumbled soy sausage patties can be substituted for the "Chorizo" if desired.*

6 SERVINGS

   1 cup chopped tomato
   1/2 cup sliced green onions and tops
   2–3 teaspoons finely chopped serrano or jalapeño chilies
   2 small cloves garlic, minced
      "Chorizo" (recipe follows)
   1 tablespoon olive oil
   6–8 eggs
   3 tablespoons reduced-fat milk
      Salt and pepper, to taste
   3/4 cup mild or hot salsa
   6 low-carb whole wheat tortillas (6-inch)

Sauté tomato, green onions, chilies, garlic, and "Chorizo" in oil in medium skillet until vegetables are tender, about 5 minutes; move mixture to side of skillet.

Beat eggs and milk until foamy; add to skillet and cook over medium to medium-low heat until eggs are cooked, stirring occasionally, 5 to 8 minutes. Stir gently into vegetable mixture and season to taste with salt and pepper. Serve with salsa and tortillas.

"Chorizo"

MAKES ABOUT 1½ CUPS

$\frac{1}{2}$ teaspoon coriander seeds, crushed

$\frac{1}{2}$ teaspoon cumin seeds, crushed

$\frac{1}{2}$–1 dried ancho chili

$\frac{1}{2}$ package (12 ounce-size) pre-browned vegetable protein crumbles

1 egg

1 tablespoon cider vinegar

1 clove garlic, minced

1 tablespoon paprika

$\frac{3}{4}$–1 teaspoon dried oregano leaves

$\frac{1}{2}$ teaspoon salt

Heat seeds in small skillet over medium heat until toasted, stirring frequently. Remove from skillet. Add chili to skillet; cook over medium heat until softened, turning frequently so chili doesn't burn, 1 to 2 minutes. Remove and discard stem, veins, and seeds. Chop chili finely.

Combine vegetable protein crumbles, seeds, chili, and remaining ingredients in bowl.

PER SERVING

Net Carbohydrate (gm): 9.9
Calories: 228.8
Fat (gm): 10.9

Saturated Fat (gm): 2.3
Cholesterol (mg): 247.4
Sodium (mg): 874

Protein (gm): 19.5
Carbohydrate (gm): 21.3

Rajas with Eggs

L-O *This Mexican-style version of hash brown potatoes is sure to please.*

4 SERVINGS

1 $1/2$ cups sliced poblano chilies or green bell peppers
$1/2$ cup sliced onion
2 tablespoons canola oil
2 cups cubed, cooked Idaho potatoes
Salt and pepper, to taste
$1/4$ cup (1 ounce) shredded Pepper-Jack cheese
8 fried or poached eggs
$1/2$ cup mild or hot salsa

Sauté chilies and onion in oil in large skillet until softened, about
5 minutes; add potatoes and cook over medium heat until potatoes are
browned, 5 to 8 minutes. Season to taste with salt and pepper; stir in
cheese. Spoon onto plates and top with eggs; serve with salsa.

....

PER SERVING
Net Carbohydrate (gm): 26.9   Saturated Fat (gm): 6.0   Protein (gm): 17.5
Calories: 396.3   Cholesterol (mg): 427.9   Carbohydrate (gm): 29.3
Fat (gm): 23.6   Sodium (mg): 479

Huevos Rancheros

o	*Serve a side dish of guacamole with this entrée for a home version of your favorite Mexican restaurant.*

6 SERVINGS

  6 low-carb whole wheat tortillas (6-inch)
 12 eggs, fried
     Salt and pepper, to taste
     Chili Tomato Sauce (recipe follows)

Cook tortillas in greased large skillet over medium heat until warm, about 1 minute on each side. Arrange tortillas on plates and top with eggs. Spoon Chili Tomato Sauce over.

Chili Tomato Sauce

MAKES ABOUT 2 CUPS

   2 cups cubed tomatoes
 $^1/_3$ cup finely chopped onion
   1 serrano or jalapeño chili, seeds and veins discarded, minced
   1 clove garlic, minced
 1–2 teaspoons olive oil
     Salt, to taste

Process tomatoes in food processor or blender until almost smooth.

Sauté onion, chili, and garlic in oil in medium skillet until tender, 3 to 4 minutes. Add tomatoes and heat to boiling; cook over medium to medium-high heat until mixture thickens to a medium sauce consistency, 5 to 8 minutes. Season to taste with salt; serve warm.

··

PER SERVING

Net Carbohydrate (gm): 6.4
Calories: 257
Fat (gm): 17.0

Saturated Fat (gm): 4.1
Cholesterol (mg): 420.4
Sodium (mg): 371

Protein (gm): 18.2
Carbohydrate (gm): 15.3

CHAPTER FOUR

Suppers

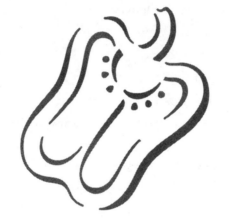

Spinach Cheese Crepes

L-O For variation, serve the crepes with *Cream Cheese Hollandaise Sauce* (see p. 67).

4 SERVINGS (2 CREPES EACH)

- $1/4$ cup chopped onion
- 2 teaspoons butter
- 1 package (10 ounces) frozen chopped spinach, thawed, well drained
- 1 cup small curd cottage cheese
- $1/4$ teaspoon dried thyme leaves
- 2–3 pinches ground nutmeg
- Salt and pepper, to taste
- 8 slices ($1/2$–$3/4$ ounce each) mozzarella or Swiss cheese
- Whole Wheat Crepes (see p. 89), warm
- Fresh Tomato and Herb Sauce (recipe follows)

Sauté onion in butter in medium skillet until tender, 3 to 4 minutes; add spinach and cook until mixture is very dry, about 5 minutes. Remove from heat and mix in cottage cheese, thyme, and nutmeg; season to taste with salt and pepper.

Place 1 cheese slice on each crepe; spoon spinach-cheese mixture along centers of crepes. Roll up and place, seam sides down, in lightly greased baking pan. Bake, loosely covered, at 325 degrees until filling is hot and cheese melted, about 10 minutes.

Arrange crepes on plates; spoon Fresh Tomato and Herb Sauce over.

Fresh Tomato and Herb Sauce

MAKES 1½ CUPS

¼ cup finely chopped onion

2 cloves garlic, minced

2 teaspoons olive oil

2½ cups peeled, seeded, chopped tomatoes

1 tablespoon finely chopped fresh or 1½ teaspoons dried basil leaves

1½ teaspoons finely chopped fresh or ¼ teaspoon dried thyme leaves

1 bay leaf

Salt and pepper, to taste

Sauté onion and garlic in oil in medium saucepan until tender, about 5 minutes. Add tomatoes and herbs to saucepan. Cook, covered, over medium-high heat until tomatoes release liquid and begin to wilt, about 5 minutes. Reduce heat and simmer, uncovered, until mixture is very thick, about 20 minutes. Discard bay leaf; season to taste with salt and pepper.

PER SERVING

Net Carbohydrate (gm): 20.4	Saturated Fat (gm): 9.5	Protein (gm): 26.9
Calories: 398.8	Cholesterol (mg): 141.4	Carbohydrate (gm): 26.2
Fat (gm): 22.2	Sodium (mg): 762	

Melted Swiss and Vegetable Crepes

L-O *The crepes are also delicious served with Wild Mushroom Sauce (see p. 91).*

4 SERVINGS (2 CREPES EACH)

   2 cups thinly sliced cabbage

   1 cup thinly sliced celery

  1/2 cup thinly sliced green bell pepper

  1/2 cup sliced mushrooms

  1/3 cup chopped green onions and tops

   1 tablespoon canola oil

2-3 teaspoons light brown sugar

   2 tablespoons water

2-3 teaspoons lemon juice

    Salt and pepper, to taste

    Whole Wheat Crepes (recipe follows), warmed

   1 cup (4 ounces) shredded Swiss cheese

Sauté cabbage, celery, bell pepper, mushrooms, and green onions in oil in large skillet 5 minutes; add sugar and water and cook, covered, over medium heat until cabbage and mushrooms are wilted, about 5 minutes. Cook, uncovered, until vegetables are tender, about 5 minutes longer. Season to taste with lemon juice, salt, and pepper.

Spoon vegetable mixture along centers of crepes; roll up and arrange, seam sides down, on broiler pan. Sprinkle tops of crepes with cheese. Broil, 6 inches from heat source, until cheese is melted, 2 to 3 minutes.

Whole Wheat Crepes

MAKES 8

   $1/2$ cup whole wheat pastry flour

   $1/2$ cup reduced-fat milk

   2 eggs

   1 tablespoon canola oil or melted butter

   $1/3$ teaspoon salt

Combine all ingredients in small bowl, beating until smooth (batter will be very thin).

Pour scant $1/4$ cup batter into greased 8-inch crepe pan or small skillet, tilting pan to coat bottom evenly with batter. Cook over medium heat until browned on the bottom, 2 to 3 minutes. Turn crepe and cook until browned on other side, 2 to 3 minutes.

PER SERVING

Net Carbohydrate (gm): 16.0   Saturated Fat (gm): 6.2   Protein (gm): 15.5

Calories: 303.6   Cholesterol (mg): 133.5   Carbohydrate (gm): 19.8

Fat (gm): 18.5   Sodium (mg): 289

Vegetable Strudel with Wild Mushroom Sauce

L-0   *A perfect dish for special occasions.*

4 SERVINGS

    1 cup chopped red and yellow bell peppers

  1/4 cup chopped shallots

    2 cloves garlic, minced

    1 tablespoon butter

1 1/2 cups broccoli florets, cooked

    1 cup cubed butternut or acorn squash, cooked

    1 cup sliced kale

      Wild Mushroom Sauce (recipe follows), divided

    1 cup (4 ounces) shredded Gruyere or Swiss cheese

      Salt and pepper, to taste

    5 sheets frozen fillo pastry, thawed

    1 tablespoon canola oil

    1 egg white

      Fresh tarragon or parsley sprigs, as garnish

Sauté bell peppers, shallots, and garlic in butter in large skillet until tender, 5 to 8 minutes. Stir in broccoli, squash, kale, and half the Wild Mushroom Sauce; cook until hot through, 2 to 3 minutes. Remove from heat and stir in cheese; season to taste with salt and pepper.

Lay 1 sheet of fillo on clean towel on table; brush lightly with combined oil and egg white. Cover with second sheet of fillo and brush with egg white mixture; repeat with remaining fillo.

Spoon vegetable mixture along long edge of fillo, 3 to 4 inches from the edge. Fold edge of fillo over filling and roll up, using towel to help lift and roll; place seam side down on greased cookie sheet. Brush top of fillo with remaining egg white mixture.

Bake at 375 degrees until golden, about 30 minutes. Let stand 5 minutes before cutting. Cut strudel into 4 pieces and arrange on plates. Spoon remaining Wild Mushroom Sauce over or alongside each serving. Garnish with tarragon sprigs.

Wild Mushroom Sauce

MAKES ABOUT 1⅓ CUPS

- 2 tablespoons finely chopped shallots
- 2 cloves garlic, minced
- 1 tablespoon butter
- 1 cup chopped or sliced wild mushrooms (portobello, shiitake, cremini, etc.)
- 2 tablespoons dry sherry or vegetable broth
- 1–2 tablespoons lemon juice
- ¼–½ teaspoon dried thyme leaves
- 1 cup vegetable broth
- 1 tablespoon cornstarch
- Salt and pepper, to taste

Sauté shallots and garlic in butter in medium saucepan until tender, 3 to 4 minutes. Stir in mushrooms; cook, covered, over medium-low heat until mushrooms are wilted, about 5 minutes. Stir in sherry, lemon juice, and thyme; heat to boiling. Reduce heat and simmer, uncovered, until mushrooms are tender and excess liquid is gone, about 5 minutes.

Mix broth and cornstarch; stir into saucepan and heat to boiling. Boil, stirring constantly, until thickened, about 1 minute. Season to taste with salt and pepper.

....

PER SERVING

Net Carbohydrate (gm): 27.7	Saturated Fat (gm): 9.0	Protein (gm): 14.8
Calories: 369.6	Cholesterol (mg): 46.9	Carbohydrate (gm): 31.6
Fat (gm): 20.5	Sodium (mg): 406	

Baked Vegetable Puff

L-O *Mushroom Toast is a flavorful accompaniment for this dish; Garlic Bread or Parmesan Toast (see pp. 48, 76) would also be excellent choices.*

6 SERVINGS

2 cups sliced mushrooms

$^1/_2$ cup chopped red bell pepper

$^1/_4$ cup finely chopped shallots

2 cloves garlic, minced

1 tablespoon canola oil

1 pound broccoli, cooked, coarsely chopped

1 cup chopped carrots, cooked

$^1/_2$ cup frozen whole kernel corn, thawed

2 teaspoons lemon juice

$^3/_4$ teaspoon dried thyme leaves

$^1/_2$ teaspoon salt

$^1/_2$ teaspoon pepper

1 cup reduced-fat milk

2 tablespoons all-purpose flour

4 eggs, lightly beaten

4 egg whites

$^1/_2$ teaspoon cream of tartar

Mushroom Toast (see p. 5)

Sauté mushrooms, bell pepper, shallots, and garlic in oil in large skillet until tender, about 4 minutes. Stir in broccoli, carrots, corn, lemon juice, thyme, salt, and pepper; sauté 5 minutes longer. Transfer vegetables to large bowl.

Whisk milk and flour in small saucepan until smooth. Heat to boiling; boil, whisking constantly, until thickened, about 1 minute. Whisk milk mixture into whole eggs in large bowl; stir in vegetable mixture.

Beat egg whites in large mixing bowl until foamy. Add cream of tartar and continue beating until stiff, but not dry, peaks form; fold into vegetable mixture and spoon all into lightly greased 1$^1\!/_2$-quart casserole. Place casserole in a large roasting pan on center rack of oven; add 2 inches hot water to pan.

Bake, uncovered, at 375 degrees 35 minutes or until casserole is puffed and lightly browned on top. Serve with Mushroom Toast.

PER SERVING

Net Carbohydrate (gm): 20.3	Saturated Fat (gm): 2.0	Protein (gm): 16.4
Calories: 256.0	Cholesterol (mg): 144.3	Carbohydrate (gm): 27.1
Fat (gm): 10.8	Sodium (mg): 469	

Veggie Stuffed Bakers and "Brats"

L For convenience, this recipe can be prepared up to 1 day in advance; refrigerate, covered. Increase baking time by about 15 minutes.

6 SERVINGS

3	medium Idaho potatoes (about 5 ounces each)
$1/2$	cup thinly sliced green onions and tops
$1/2$	cup chopped red bell pepper
4	cloves garlic, minced
1	tablespoon canola oil
$1/2$	cup sour cream
1	cup (4 ounces) shredded Cheddar cheese, divided
	Salt and pepper, to taste
1	cup broccoli florets, cooked until crisp-tender
$1 1/2$	packages (10-ounce size) soy brats, cooked

Grease potatoes lightly and pierce in several places with a fork; bake at 400 degrees until tender, 45 to 60 minutes. Let stand until cool enough to handle. Cut potatoes lengthwise into halves; scoop out insides of potatoes (leaving shells intact) and mash.

Sauté green onions, bell pepper, and garlic in oil in medium skillet until tender, about 5 minutes. Mix vegetables, sour cream and $1/2$ cup cheese into mashed potatoes and season to taste with salt and pepper. Spoon mixture into potato shells; arrange broccoli on top and sprinkle with remaining cheese.

Arrange potatoes in baking pan; bake, uncovered, at 350 degrees until hot through, 20 to 30 minutes. Serve with soy brats.

PER SERVING

Net Carbohydrate (gm): 17.5
Calories: 339.7
Fat (gm): 19.1

Saturated Fat (gm): 6.8
Cholesterol (mg): 26.8
Sodium (mg): 1008

Protein (gm): 18.8
Carbohydrate (gm): 22.0

Rice-Stuffed Tomatoes with Cheese and Spinach Squares

L-0 | *Make the Cheese and Spinach Squares first, then prepare the tomatoes while they are baking.*

6 SERVINGS

6 large tomatoes (about 2 pounds)
1 cup chopped mushrooms
3/4 cup sliced green onions and tops
2 tablespoons olive or canola oil
2 cups cooked brown rice
1 1/2 teaspoons dried Italian seasoning
Salt and pepper, to taste
Chopped fresh parsley, as garnish
Cheese and Spinach Squares (see p. 13)

Slice 3/4 to 1 inch off top of each tomato. Scoop out pulp; coarsely chop tops and pulp.

Sauté mushrooms and green onions in oil in medium skillet until tender, about 8 minutes. Stir in chopped tomatoes, rice, and Italian seasoning; season to taste with salt and pepper. Spoon mixture into tomato shells and arrange in lightly greased baking pan. Bake, loosely covered, at 350 degrees until hot through, about 20 minutes. Sprinkle with parsley and serve with Cheese and Spinach Squares.

....

PER SERVING

Net Carbohydrate (gm): 23.0	Saturated Fat (gm): 5.1	Protein (gm): 14.0
Calories: 274.0	Cholesterol (mg): 55.3	Carbohydrate (gm): 27.6
Fat (gm): 12.8	Sodium (mg): 280	

Stuffed Tomato Halves, Red and Yellow

L *Mushrooms, spinach, rice, and cheese are combined for a flavorful filling in this colorful dish.*

4 SERVINGS

  4 ounces mushrooms, chopped
 1/4 cup sliced green onions and tops
  1 tablespoon butter
 1/2 package (10-ounce size) frozen chopped spinach, thawed, drained
  3 tablespoons all-purpose flour
  1 cup reduced-fat milk
 1/4 teaspoon dried tarragon leaves
 1-2 pinches ground nutmeg
  1 cup cooked brown rice
  1 cup (4 ounces) shredded Cheddar or Swiss cheese, divided
   Salt and pepper, to taste
  2 large red tomatoes
  2 large yellow tomatoes
   Fresh parsley, minced, as garnish
  4 slices Garlic Bread (1/2 recipe) (see p. 48)

Sauté mushrooms and green onions in butter in large skillet until tender, 5 to 8 minutes. Stir in spinach; cook until hot, 3 to 4 minutes. Stir in flour; cook 1 to 2 minutes longer.

Stir milk, tarragon, and nutmeg into vegetable mixture and heat to boiling; reduce heat and simmer 2 to 3 minutes. Remove from heat and stir in rice and 1/2 cup cheese; season to taste with salt and pepper.

Cut tomatoes crosswise into halves; remove seeds and hollow out slightly. Chop removed portions of tomato and stir into filling. Spoon filling into tomatoes and place in lightly greased baking pan.

Bake tomatoes at 375 degrees until hot through, 15 to 20 minutes, sprinkling with remaining $1/2$ cup cheese during last 5 minutes of baking. Arrange 1 yellow and 1 red tomato half on each plate; sprinkle with parsley. Serve with Garlic Bread.

PER SERVING

Net Carbohydrate (gm): 29.1	Saturated Fat (gm): 10.7	Protein (gm): 18.9
Calories: 392.2	Cholesterol (mg): 54.7	Carbohydrate (gm): 36.1
Fat (gm): 20.9	Sodium (mg): 446	

Grilled Vegetable Rollups

L-O *Vegetables can be grilled and roll-ups assembled a day in advance; refrigerate, covered. When ready to use, increase baking time to 40 to 45 minutes.*

8 SERVINGS (2 ROLLUPS EACH)

1 large eggplant (1 1/4 pounds), unpeeled, cut lengthwise into scant 1/2-inch-thick slices (8 slices)

2 large zucchini, cut lengthwise into scant 1/2-inch-thick slices (8 slices)

Vegetable cooking spray

2 teaspoons finely chopped fresh parsley

1 teaspoon dried basil leaves

1/2 teaspoon dried oregano leaves

1/2 teaspoon black pepper

1/2 teaspoon crushed red pepper

2 cups ricotta cheese

1/4 cup (1 ounce) grated Parmesan cheese

Salt, to taste

1 egg

Roasted Tomato-Herb Sauce (recipe follows)

1 1/2 cups (6 ounces) shredded mozzarella cheese

Spray eggplant and zucchini with cooking spray; sprinkle with 1/2 the combined herbs and black and red pepper. Grill vegetables on greased rack over medium-hot coals until softened, turning once, about 5 minutes.

Combine ricotta and Parmesan cheeses with remaining herbs and black and red pepper; season to taste with salt. Mix in egg.

Spread about 2 tablespoons cheese mixture on each eggplant and zucchini slice and roll up. Spread about 1 cup Roasted Tomato-Herb Sauce in bottom of 13 x 9-inch baking pan. Arrange vegetable rolls, seam sides down, in pan. Spoon remaining 2 cups Roasted Tomato-Herb Sauce over rolls; sprinkle with mozzarella cheese. Bake, uncovered, at 350 degrees 30 minutes.

Roasted Tomato-Herb Sauce

MAKES ABOUT 3 CUPS

$2^1/_2$ cups halved Italian plum tomatoes

    1 leek (white part only), cut into $^3/_4$-inch pieces

    1 cup onion wedges

    1 cup carrot pieces ($^3/_4$-inch)

    3 cloves garlic, peeled

    2 tablespoons olive oil

    $^1/_2$ teaspoon dried oregano leaves

    $^1/_4$ teaspoon dried marjoram leaves

    $^1/_8$ teaspoon pepper

    $^1/_2$ cup loosely packed fresh basil leaves

    Salt and pepper, to taste

Line large jelly roll pan with aluminum foil and grease lightly. Arrange vegetables and garlic in single layer on pan; drizzle with olive oil and sprinkle with oregano, marjoram, and pepper. Roast at 425 degrees until vegetables are browned and tender, about 40 minutes.

Process vegetables and fresh basil in food processor or blender until almost smooth. Season to taste with salt and pepper.

....

PER SERVING

Net Carbohydrate (gm): 11.2	Saturated Fat (gm): 8.9	Protein (gm): 16.5
Calories: 275.7	Cholesterol (mg): 71.4	Carbohydrate (gm): 16.0
Fat (gm): 17.7	Sodium (mg): 266	

Eggplant and Tomato Sauce Parmesan

Eggplant layered with Tomato and "Meat" Sauce and melted cheese is baked to rich goodness.

6 SERVINGS

>   2 large eggplant, unpeeled (about 3 pounds), cut into scant $^1/_2$-inch slices
>
>   Salt
>
> 2–4 tablespoons olive oil
>
>   Tomato and "Meat" Sauce (recipe follows)
>
> 1$^1/_2$ cups (6 ounces) shredded mozzarella cheese, divided
>
> $^1/_2$ cup (2 ounces) grated Parmesan cheese

Sprinkle eggplant slices lightly with salt; let stand 30 minutes. Rinse thoroughly and drain on paper toweling.

Line large jelly roll pan with aluminum foil and grease lightly. Arrange eggplant in single layer on pan; brush lightly with oil. Bake at 425 degrees until tender, 20 to 30 minutes.

Layer $^1/_3$ of eggplant slices, 1$^1/_3$ cups Tomato and "Meat" Sauce, and $^1/_2$ cup mozzarella cheese in greased 13 x 9-inch baking pan. Repeat layers 2 times; sprinkle with Parmesan cheese. Bake, uncovered, at 350 degrees until bubbly, 30 to 40 minutes. Cool 10 minutes before cutting.

Tomato and "Meat" Sauce

MAKES ABOUT 1 QUART

$^1/_2$ cup chopped onion

3 cloves garlic, minced

2 teaspoons olive oil

1 can (28 ounces) reduced-sodium diced tomatoes, undrained

$^1/_2$ package (12-ounce size) frozen pre-browned vegetable
   protein crumbles

$^1/_3$ cup finely chopped fresh parsley

$^1/_4$ cup water

$^3/_4$ teaspoon dried Italian seasoning

$^3/_4$ teaspoon dried basil leaves

$^1/_2$ teaspoon dried oregano leaves

$^1/_8$ teaspoon ground nutmeg

Salt and pepper, to taste

Sauté onion and garlic in oil in large saucepan until tender, 3 to 5 minutes.
Add remaining ingredients, except salt and pepper; heat to boiling. Reduce
heat and simmer, uncovered, until thickened, about 20 minutes, stirring
occasionally. Season to taste with salt and pepper.

PER SERVING

Net Carbohydrate (gm): 13.8   Saturated Fat (gm): 5.6   Protein (gm): 19.4
Calories: 295.1   Cholesterol (mg): 20.9   Carbohydrate (gm): 24.6
Fat (gm): 14.7   Sodium (mg): 524

Eggplant and Zucchini Casserole

L **Herb-seasoned and baked with a tomato-cheese topping, this casserole
is both flavorful and healthful.**

4 SERVINGS

- 1 large eggplant (1¼ pounds), unpeeled, cut into ½-inch slices
- 4 medium zucchini, cut in half lengthwise
- 1 cup sliced green bell pepper (¾-inch)
- 2 tablespoons olive oil
- ½ teaspoon dried marjoram leaves
- ½ teaspoon dried oregano leaves
- ¼ teaspoon garlic powder
- ⅛–¼ teaspoon crushed red pepper
  Salt and pepper, to taste
- 2 cups coarsely chopped tomatoes
- ½ cup pine nuts, toasted
- ¼ cup sliced ripe or Greek olives
- 1 package (8 ounces) cream cheese, room temperature
- ¼ cup reduced-fat milk
- 2 tablespoons reduced-sodium tomato paste
  Salt and pepper, to taste
- 1½ cups (6 ounces) shredded Cheddar cheese

Line large jelly roll pan with aluminum foil and grease lightly. Arrange
eggplant, zucchini, and bell pepper on pan; drizzle with oil and sprinkle
with marjoram, oregano, garlic powder, and crushed red pepper.

Roast vegetables at 475 degrees until beginning to brown, 15 to 20 minutes.
Sprinkle lightly with salt and pepper. Arrange roasted vegetables in greased
11 x 7-inch baking dish. Sprinkle tomatoes, pine nuts, and olives over top.

Combine cream cheese, milk, and tomato paste in small saucepan; heat
over low heat until cheese is melted, stirring constantly. Season to taste
with salt and pepper and pour over vegetables; sprinkle with shredded
cheese. Bake at 375 degrees 15 minutes, or until vegetables are tender.

....

PER SERVING

Net Carbohydrate (gm): 16.5	Saturated Fat (gm): 23.5	Protein (gm): 22.6
Calories: 651.0	Cholesterol (mg): 107.0	Carbohydrate (gm): 26.6
Fat (gm): 54.2	Sodium (mg): 541	

Zucchini and Mushrooms Parmesan

L *For color contrast, substitute yellow summer squash for part of the zucchini in this dish.*

4 SERVINGS

1 1/2 pounds zucchini, cut lengthwise into 1/8-inch slices
  2 large portobello or shiitake mushrooms, sliced
  1 pound plum tomatoes, thinly sliced
    Salt and pepper, to taste
  1/2 cup finely chopped onion
  3 cloves garlic, minced
  1 teaspoon dried basil leaves
  1/2 teaspoon dried marjoram leaves
1/4–1/2 teaspoon crushed red pepper
  1 1/2 cups (6 ounces) shredded mozzarella cheese
  1/4 cup (1 ounce) shredded Parmesan cheese

Layer zucchini, mushrooms, and tomatoes in lightly greased 11 x 7-inch baking dish; sprinkle lightly with salt and pepper. Sprinkle onion, garlic, basil, marjoram, and crushed red pepper over vegetables.

Combine cheeses and sprinkle over vegetable mixture. Bake, uncovered, at 350 degrees 30 minutes or until vegetables are tender.

PER SERVING

Net Carbohydrate (gm): 11.7   Saturated Fat (gm): 6.2   Protein (gm): 16.2
Calories: 206.1   Cholesterol (mg): 26.9   Carbohydrate (gm): 15.7
Fat (gm): 11.1   Sodium (mg): 386

Southern Stewed Black Eyes

V	*A hearty stew that can be made in less than 30 minutes! You can find soy sausage links in the refrigerated produce and frozen sections of the grocery store.*

6 SERVINGS (ABOUT 1¼ CUPS EACH)

$^1/_2$ cup chopped onion

2 cloves garlic, minced

$^1/_2$ package (10-ounce size) soy sausage links, cut into $^3/_4$-inch pieces

1 tablespoon olive oil

2 cups fresh or frozen okra, cut into 1-inch pieces

1 can (16 ounces) reduced-sodium whole tomatoes, undrained, coarsely chopped

2 cans (15 ounces each) black-eyed peas, rinsed, drained

$^1/_2$ package (10-ounce size) frozen spinach, partially thawed

1 teaspoon dried marjoram leaves

$^3/_4$ teaspoon dried thyme leaves

$^1/_4$ teaspoon hot pepper sauce

Salt and pepper, to taste

Sauté onion, garlic, and soy sausage in oil in large saucepan until onion is tender, 5 to 8 minutes. Stir in remaining ingredients, except salt and pepper; heat to boiling. Reduce heat and simmer, covered, until okra is tender, 10 to 15 minutes. Season to taste with salt and pepper.

....

PER SERVING

Net Carbohydrate (gm): 20.8   Saturated Fat (gm): 0.7   Protein (gm): 14.0
Calories: 203.2   Cholesterol (mg): 0.0   Carbohydrate (gm): 28.1
Fat (gm): 4.2   Sodium (mg): 480

Black Bean and Okra Gumbo

V
For easier preparation, substitute 2 cans (15 ounces each) rinsed and drained black beans for the dried.

8 SERVINGS (ABOUT 1 CUP EACH)

2 cups halved small mushrooms

1½ cups chopped red and green bell peppers

1 cup chopped onion

1 cup sliced carrots

2 tablespoons olive oil

1 tablespoon chili powder

1 teaspoon gumbo filé powder

2 cups vegetable broth

1 can (16 ounces) tomatoes with chilies, undrained

3 cups cooked dried black beans

2 cups fresh or frozen cut okra

1 package (10 ounces) soy sausage, cut into ½-inch pieces

Salt and pepper, to taste

Sauté mushrooms, bell peppers, onion, and carrots in oil in large skillet until mushrooms and onions are tender, about 10 minutes. Stir in chili powder and filé powder; cook 2 to 3 minutes.

Add broth, tomatoes with liquid, beans, okra, and sausage; heat to boiling. Reduce heat and simmer, covered until vegetables are tender, about 10 minutes. Simmer, uncovered, until thickened to desired consistency, 5 to 10 minutes. Season to taste with salt and pepper.

PER SERVING

Net Carbohydrate (gm): 19.5	Saturated Fat (gm): 0.9	Protein (gm): 14.3
Calories: 230.7	Cholesterol (mg): 0.0	Carbohydrate (gm): 29.6
Fat (gm): 6.8	Sodium (mg): 722	

Easy Creole Skillet Stew

V	*No time to cook? This easy stew can be on the table in less than 30 minutes!*

4 SERVINGS

1 package (10 ounces) soy sausage links

$^3/_4$ cup chopped onion

2 cloves garlic, minced

1 tablespoon olive oil

1 $^1/_2$ cups sliced zucchini

$^3/_4$ cup fresh or frozen whole kernel corn

2 tablespoons all-purpose flour

$^1/_2$ teaspoon dried thyme leaves

$^1/_2$ teaspoon dried sage leaves

1 can (28 ounces) reduced-sodium stewed tomatoes, undrained

Salt and pepper, to taste

2 green onions and tops, sliced

Sauté soy sausage, onion, and garlic in oil in large skillet until onion is tender and soy sausage browned, 5 to 8 minutes. Add zucchini and corn to skillet and sauté 3 to 4 minutes. Stir in flour and herbs; cook 1 to 2 minutes longer. Add tomatoes and liquid and heat to boiling; boil, stirring, until thickened, 1 to 2 minutes. Season to taste with salt and pepper; sprinkle with green onions.

PER SERVING

Net Carbohydrate (gm): 23.6	Saturated Fat (gm): 1.3	Protein (gm): 18.4
Calories: 274.1	Cholesterol (mg): 0.0	Carbohydrate (gm): 31.3
Fat (gm): 9.0	Sodium (mg): 562	

Tacos Picadillo

This Mexican favorite is seasoned with raisins, almonds, sweet spices, and jalapeño chili.

6 SERVINGS (1 TACO EACH)

$^1/_4$ cup chopped onion

2 cloves garlic, minced

$^1/_2$ small jalapeño chili, seeds and veins discarded, minced

1 teaspoon canola oil

$^3/_4$ package (12-ounce size) frozen pre-browned vegetable protein crumbles, thawed

$^1/_2$ cup chopped tomato

$^1/_4$ cup dark raisins

$^1/_4$ cup slivered almonds, toasted

1–2 teaspoons cider vinegar

1 teaspoon ground cinnamon

$^3/_4$ teaspoon dried oregano leaves

$^1/_4$ teaspoon ground cloves

$^1/_4$ teaspoon ground allspice

Salt and pepper, to taste

6 low-carb whole wheat tortillas, warmed

Tomato Poblano Salsa (recipe follows)

Sauté onion, garlic, and jalapeño chili in oil in medium skillet until tender, about 5 minutes. Add vegetable protein crumbles, tomato, raisins, almonds, vinegar, cinnamon, oregano, cloves, and allspice. Cook over medium heat, stirring occasionally, until mixture is hot through, about 5 minutes. Season to taste with salt and pepper.

Spoon about $^1/_3$ cup mixture on each tortilla and roll up. Serve with Tomato-Poblano Salsa.

Tomato-Poblano Salsa

MAKES ABOUT 1 CUP

$^3/_4$ cup chopped tomato

$^1/_4$ cup chopped poblano chili

3 tablespoons chopped cilantro

2 tablespoons finely chopped onion

1 teaspoon finely chopped jalapeño chili (seeds and veins discarded)

1 clove garlic, minced

Salt, to taste

Mix all ingredients, except salt; season to taste with salt.

PER SERVING
Net Carbohydrate (gm): 14.3
Calories: 188.2
Fat (gm): 6.1

Saturated Fat (gm): 0.3
Cholesterol (mg): 0.0
Sodium (mg): 469

Protein (gm): 16.2
Carbohydrate (gm): 27.2

Tacos with "Chorizo" and Potatoes

L In many parts of Mexico, fried tacos are made by pan-sautéing folded, filled tortillas—a delectable alternative to the crisp fried taco shells we are accustomed to.

8 SERVINGS (1 TACO EACH)

1 cup chopped onion

1 cup cubed, peeled, cooked potato

1 tablespoon canola oil

"Chorizo" (see p. 81)

2 cups Tomato-Poblano Salsa (double recipe) (see p. 108), divided

1 cup (4 ounces) shredded Cheddar cheese

2 tablespoons finely chopped cilantro

Salt and pepper, to taste

8 low-carb whole wheat tortillas

$1/4$ cup sour cream

Sauté onion and potato in oil in large skillet until onion is tender and potatoes browned, about 5 minutes. Stir in "Chorizo" and $1/2$ cup Tomato-Poblano Salsa; cook 1 to 2 minutes longer. Remove from heat; stir in cheese and cilantro. Season to taste with salt and pepper.

Heat tortillas in skillet or microwave oven until softened. Spoon about $1/2$ cup vegetable mixture on each tortilla and fold in half. Cook tacos in greased large skillet until lightly browned, 1 to 2 minutes on each side. Serve with remaining $1\,1/2$ cups Tomato-Poblano Salsa and sour cream.

PER SERVING

Net Carbohydrate (gm): 13.4   Saturated Fat (gm): 4.1   Protein (gm): 15.5
Calories: 221.4   Cholesterol (mg): 43.9   Carbohydrate (gm): 24.8
Fat (gm): 10.9   Sodium (mg): 573

Tempeh Steak with Red and Green Stir-Fry

| v |

If available, use red Swiss chard for its beautiful red and green color.

6 SERVINGS

1 cup sliced red onions
1 cup sliced celery
2 teaspoons minced garlic
1 teaspoon minced gingerroot
1 tablespoon canola oil
6 cups shredded red or green Swiss chard or spinach
2 cups sliced red and green bell peppers
2 cups vegetable broth
2 tablespoons cornstarch
4 teaspoons reduced-sodium tamari soy sauce
$^1/_2$–$^3/_4$ teaspoon hot chili paste
Salt and pepper, to taste
3 packages (8 ounces each) tempeh or firm tofu, cut into halves

Stir-fry onions, celery, garlic, and gingerroot in oil in wok or large skillet 1 to 2 minutes. Add Swiss chard and stir-fry 1 to 2 minutes. Add bell peppers to wok; stir-fry until vegetables are crisp-tender, 2 to 3 minutes.

Combine broth, cornstarch, soy sauce, and chili paste; stir into wok. Heat to boiling; boil, stirring constantly, until thickened, about 1 minute. Season to taste with salt and pepper.

Cook tempeh over medium heat in greased large skillet until browned, 2 to 3 minutes on each side. Arrange tempeh on serving platter; spoon vegetable mixture over.

PER SERVING

Net Carbohydrate (gm): 19.4	Saturated Fat (gm): 2.7	Protein (gm): 23.3
Calories: 294.0	Cholesterol (mg): 0.0	Carbohydrate (gm): 22.0
Fat (gm): 15.0	Sodium (mg): 396	

Grilled Tempeh with Poblano Sour Cream Sauce

L *Poblano Sour Cream Sauce adds a flavor of the Southwest.*

6 SERVINGS

- $1/3$ cup lime juice
- 4 cloves garlic, minced
- $1 1/2$ teaspoons dried oregano leaves
- $1/2$ teaspoon ground allspice
- $1/4$ teaspoon pepper
- 3 packages (8 ounces each) tempeh or firm tofu cut crosswise into halves
- 2 tablespoons olive oil

  Poblano Sour Cream Sauce (recipe follows)

  Cilantro, finely chopped, as garnish

Combine lime juice, garlic, oregano, allspice, and pepper; pour over tempeh in shallow glass baking dish. Refrigerate 1 to 2 hours, turning tempeh occasionally; drain.

Brush tempeh on both sides with oil. Grill, covered, on greased rack over medium-hot coals until tempeh is browned, 4 to 6 minutes on each side.

Arrange tempeh on plates; spoon Poblano Sour Cream Sauce over and garnish with cilantro.

Poblano Sour Cream Sauce

MAKES ABOUT 1½ CUPS

1 cup thinly sliced poblano chili
¼ cup chopped onion
2 cloves garlic, minced
2 teaspoons olive oil
1 cup sour cream
¼–½ teaspoon ground cumin
Salt and pepper, to taste

Sauté poblano chili, onion, and garlic in oil in medium skillet until very tender, about 10 minutes. Stir in sour cream and cumin; cook over low heat until hot, 2 to 3 minutes. Season to taste with salt and pepper.

PER SERVING

Net Carbohydrate (gm): 17.9	Saturated Fat (gm): 7.5	Protein (gm): 23.2
Calories: 368.0	Cholesterol (mg): 14.1	Carbohydrate (gm): 18.5
Fat (gm): 25.2	Sodium (mg): 31	

Garden Vegetable and Tempeh Sauté

[V] *Vary the vegetables according to season and availability.*

4 SERVINGS

      Tamari Marinade (recipe follows)

1 package (8 ounces) tempeh or firm tofu

$1/2$ cup sliced onion

$1/2$ cup sliced red bell pepper

1 teaspoon minced garlic

1 tablespoon olive oil

2 cups sliced mushrooms

1 cup sliced zucchini

1 cup reduced-sodium tomato juice

1 teaspoon dried basil leaves

1 teaspoon dried oregano leaves

$1/4$ teaspoon cayenne pepper

$1 1/2$ cups tomato wedges

      Salt and pepper, to taste

      Fresh parsley, minced, as garnish

Pour Tamari Marinade over tempeh in shallow glass bowl; refrigerate, covered, 4 hours or overnight. Drain; reserve marinade. Cut tempeh into $1/2$-inch cubes.

Sauté onion, bell pepper, and garlic in oil in large skillet 5 minutes; add tempeh and cook until vegetables are tender and tempeh is browned, about 5 minutes.

Stir in reserved marinade and remaining ingredients, except tomato wedges, salt and pepper, and parsley; heat to boiling. Reduce heat and simmer, covered, until vegetables are tender, 5 to 8 minutes. Add tomato wedges; cook, covered, until softened, about 5 minutes. Season with salt and pepper. Sprinkle with parsley.

Tamari Marinade

MAKES 4 SERVINGS (1 TABLESPOON EACH)

2 tablespoons reduced-sodium tamari soy sauce

2 tablespoons red wine vinegar

1 1/2 teaspoons minced garlic

1 1/2 teaspoons dried Italian seasoning

Mix all ingredients.

PER SERVING

Net Carbohydrate (gm): 13.9	Saturated Fat (gm): 1.8	Protein (gm): 14.3
Calories: 197.4	Cholesterol (mg): 0.0	Carbohydrate (gm): 16.8
Fat (gm): 10.0	Sodium (mg): 321	

Vegetables and Tempeh Marengo

| V |

Flavors of the Mediterranean accent this colorful dish.

6 SERVINGS (ABOUT 1 CUP EACH)

1 1/2 packages (8-ounce size) tempeh or firm tofu, cubed
(3/4-inch)
1 tablespoon canola oil
2 cups cubed zucchini
1 cup onion wedges
1 cup halved small mushrooms
2 cloves minced garlic
1 tablespoon all-purpose flour
1 can (16 ounces) reduced-sodium diced tomatoes, undrained
3/4 cup vegetable broth
1 strip orange rind (3 x 1-inch)
1/2 teaspoon dried thyme leaves
1/2 teaspoon dried oregano leaves
1 bay leaf
Salt and pepper, to taste
2 cups cooked brown rice, warm

Sauté tempeh in oil in large skillet until browned, about 5 minutes; remove from skillet and reserve. Add zucchini, onion wedges, mushrooms, and garlic to skillet; sauté 5 minutes. Stir in flour and cook 1 minute longer. Add remaining ingredients, except salt and pepper, and rice; heat to boiling. Add reserved tempeh; reduce heat and simmer, covered, until vegetables are tender, about 10 minutes. Discard bay leaf; season to taste with salt and pepper. Serve over rice.

••

PER SERVING

Net Carbohydrate (gm): 26.9	Saturated Fat (gm): 1.6	Protein (gm): 14.2
Calories: 248.4	Cholesterol (mg): 0.0	Carbohydrate (gm): 30.6
Fat (gm): 9.2	Sodium (mg): 101	

Ratatouille and "Sausage"

| V | *This French vegetable stew is layered and baked the traditional way. The soy sausage can be crumbled and layered with the vegetables, if you like.* |

4 SERVINGS

2 cups sliced onions

$^1/_2$ cup sliced green bell pepper

4 cloves garlic, minced

2 tablespoons olive oil, divided

1$^1/_2$ cups coarsely chopped tomatoes

Salt and pepper, to taste

1 large eggplant (about 1 pound), unpeeled

1$^1/_2$ cups sliced zucchini

3 tablespoons minced fresh parsley

1$^1/_2$ teaspoons dried oregano leaves

1 teaspoon dried marjoram leaves

$^1/_2$ teaspoon dried thyme leaves

$^1/_2$ teaspoon dried savory leaves

1 package (10 ounces) soy Italian sausage, cooked

Sauté onions, bell pepper, and garlic in 1 tablespoon oil in large skillet until tender, about 5 minutes. Add tomatoes and cook, covered, 5 minutes; cook uncovered until excess liquid is gone, about 5 minutes. Season to taste with salt and pepper. Transfer mixture to bowl and reserve.

Cut eggplant into strips measuring about 3 x $^1/_2$ x $^1/_2$ inches. Add eggplant and zucchini to skillet and sauté in remaining 1 tablespoon oil until lightly browned. Season to taste with salt and pepper.

Combine parsley and dried herbs in bowl. Layer half the eggplant mixture in greased 1$^1/_2$-quart casserole and sprinkle with $^1/_4$ the herbs. Layer half the onion mixture over eggplant mixture and sprinkle with $^1/_4$ the herbs. Repeat layers. Bake, uncovered, at 400 degrees until hot through, 15 to 20 minutes. Serve with soy Italian sausage.

••

PER SERVING

Net Carbohydrate (gm): 18.2   Saturated Fat (gm): 1.1   Protein (gm): 14.5
Calories: 281.5   Cholesterol (mg): 0.0   Carbohydrate (gm): 28.3
Fat (gm): 13.4   Sodium (mg): 1004

Portobello Mushrooms with Sautéed Vegetables and Blue Cheese Polenta

L *Make this recipe with porcini mushrooms if you are fortunate enough to find them in season.*

4 SERVINGS

4 large portobello mushrooms (5–6 inches in diameter) (8 ounces)

2 tablespoons olive oil, divided

Salt and pepper, to taste

2 cups sliced red and yellow bell peppers

3 green onions and tops, sliced

2 cloves garlic, minced

1 cup chopped tomato

1 tablespoon balsamic vinegar

1 teaspoon dried basil leaves

$^1/_2$ teaspoon dried rosemary leaves

Blue Cheese Polenta (recipe follows)

$^1/_4$ cup pine nuts

$^1/_4$ cup (1 ounce) crumbled blue cheese

Brush mushrooms with 1 tablespoon oil; broil 6 inches from heat source, until mushrooms are tender, about 8 minutes, turning mushrooms occasionally. Sprinkle mushrooms lightly with salt and pepper.

Sauté bell peppers, green onions, and garlic in remaining 1 tablespoon oil in large skillet until tender, 5 to 8 minutes. Add tomato and cook, covered, over medium heat 5 minutes. Stir in vinegar and herbs; season to taste with salt and pepper.

Spoon Blue Cheese Polenta onto plates, arranging mushrooms on top. Spoon sautéed vegetables over mushrooms; sprinkle with pine nuts and blue cheese.

Blue Cheese Polenta

MAKES ABOUT 4 CUPS

> 4 cups water
> 1 cup yellow cornmeal
> $^3/_4$ cup (3 ounces) crumbled blue cheese
> Pepper, to taste

Heat water to boiling in large saucepan; gradually stir in cornmeal. Cook over medium to medium-low heat, stirring constantly, until polenta thickens enough to hold its shape, but is still soft, 5 to 8 minutes. Stir in blue cheese; season to taste with pepper.

PER SERVING

Net Carbohydrate (gm): 29.3	Saturated Fat (gm): 7.6	Protein (gm): 14.1
Calories: 398.3	Cholesterol (mg): 24.3	Carbohydrate (gm): 36.4
Fat (gm): 23.4	Sodium (mg): 476	

Roasted Stuffed Portobello Mushrooms with Basil Pesto

L *Serve one mushroom each if using as a first course. The vegetable stuffing can also be used to fill large white mushroom caps.*

4 SERVINGS (2 MUSHROOMS EACH)

8 large portobello mushrooms (5–6 inches in diameter) (about 1 pound)

1 cup finely chopped zucchini

1 cup shredded carrots

$1/4$ cup thinly sliced green onions and tops

1 tablespoon olive oil

$1/4$ cup dry unseasoned bread crumbs

$1/3$ cup prepared basil pesto

Salt and pepper, to taste

$1 1/2$ cups (6 ounces) shredded mozzarella cheese

4 slices low-carb whole wheat bread, toasted

4 teaspoons butter

Remove mushroom stems and chop. Sauté mushroom stems, zucchini, carrots, and green onions in oil in large skillet until crisp-tender, 8 to 10 minutes. Stir in bread crumbs and pesto. Season to taste with salt and pepper. Spoon vegetable mixture onto mushrooms.

Line large jelly roll pan with aluminum foil and grease lightly. Arrange mushrooms on pan and roast at 425 degrees until mushrooms are tender, about 20 minutes, sprinkling with cheese the last 5 minutes over roasting time.

Spread toast with butter and cut diagonally into halves; serve mushrooms on toast halves.

PER SERVING

Net Carbohydrate (gm): 21.5   Saturated Fat (gm): 9.2   Protein (gm): 20.7
Calories: 402.8   Cholesterol (mg): 44.3   Carbohydrate (gm): 28.8
Fat (gm): 24.3   Sodium (mg): 684

Savory Stuffed Portobello Mushrooms

L *These entrée-size mushrooms can also be served as appetizers; select smaller mushrooms, or cut large mushrooms into halves or quarters.*

4 SERVINGS (2 MUSHROOMS EACH)

8 large portobello mushrooms (5–6 inches in diameter) (about 1 pound)

2 cups chopped red and yellow bell peppers

$^1/_2$ cup chopped shallots or onion

$^1/_4$ cup thinly sliced green onions and tops

6 cloves garlic, minced

2 tablespoons olive oil

$^1/_2$ teaspoon dried basil leaves

$^1/_2$ teaspoon dried marjoram leaves

$^1/_4$–$^1/_2$ teaspoon dried thyme leaves

Salt and pepper, to taste

1 $^1/_2$ cups (6 ounces) shredded mozzarella or Cheddar cheese

8 slices low-carb whole wheat bread, toasted

Fresh basil or parsley sprigs, as garnish

Remove mushroom stems and chop. Sauté mushroom stems, bell peppers, shallots, green onions, and garlic in oil in large skillet until tender, 8 to 10 minutes. Stir in herbs and cook 1 to 2 minutes longer; season to taste with salt and pepper.

Spoon vegetable mixture onto mushrooms; place on jelly-roll pan. Bake, loosely covered at 425 degrees 15 minutes. Sprinkle with cheese and bake uncovered until mushrooms are tender and cheese melted, 8 to 10 minutes longer. Serve mushrooms on toast; garnish with basil or parsley.

PER SERVING

Net Carbohydrate (gm): 26.7
Calories: 375.4
Fat (gm): 19.3

Saturated Fat (gm): 6.2
Cholesterol (mg): 22.5
Sodium (mg): 558

Protein (gm): 23.1
Carbohydrate (gm): 35.9

Roasted Summer Vegetables with Pasta

[o] *For attractive serving, the pasta can be shaped into small nests to contain the medley of roasted vegetables.*

8 SERVINGS

> 3 tablespoons olive oil
>
> 2 tablespoons balsamic or red wine vinegar
>
> 1 teaspoon lemon juice
>
> 3 cloves garlic, minced
>
> 2 teaspoons crushed caraway seeds
>
> $1/4$ teaspoon salt
>
> $1/4$ teaspoon pepper
>
> 1 medium eggplant (12 ounces), peeled, cut into 1-inch pieces
>
> 1 cup sliced zucchini
>
> 1 cup sliced red or green bell pepper
>
> 1 small red onion, cut into 1-inch wedges
>
> 16 ounces low-carb whole wheat linguine, cooked, warm
>
> Minced fresh parsley, as garnish

Mix oil, vinegar, lemon juice, garlic, caraway seeds, salt, and pepper; pour over combined vegetables in shallow glass baking dish. Let stand, covered, 30 to 60 minutes.

Line large jelly roll pan with aluminum foil and grease lightly; arrange vegetables in single layer on pan. Bake at 425 degrees until vegetables are browned and tender, 30 to 40 minutes.

Toss vegetables and pasta in large serving bowl; sprinkle with parsley.

....

PER SERVING

Net Carbohydrate (gm): 28.6   Saturated Fat (gm): 0.7   Protein (gm): 17.3
Calories: 275.0   Cholesterol (mg): 0.0   Carbohydrate (gm): 37.8
Fat (gm): 6.3   Sodium (mg): 259

Creamy Fettuccine Primavera

 The sauce for this dish should be somewhat thin, as it thickens when removed from the heat. If made in advance, the sauce will require additional milk when reheating.

4 SERVINGS

- 2 cups sliced mushrooms
- 1 cup broccoli florets
- 1 cup cubed yellow summer squash
- $^1/_2$ cup chopped red bell pepper
- 2 tablespoons olive oil
- 1 package (8 ounces) cream cheese
- $^2/_3$–1 cup reduced-fat milk, divided
- $^1/_4$ cup sliced green onions and tops
- $^1/_2$ teaspoon dried Italian seasoning
- $^1/_2$ cup (2 ounces) shredded Parmesan cheese
- Salt and white pepper, to taste
- 8 ounces low-carb whole wheat fettuccine or linguine, cooked, warm

Sauté mushrooms, broccoli, squash, and bell pepper in oil in large skillet 3 to 4 minutes. Cover and cook over medium to medium-low heat until vegetables are just tender, 6 to 8 minutes.

Heat cream cheese, $^2/_3$ cup milk, green onions, and Italian seasoning in small saucepan over low heat until cream cheese is melted, stirring frequently. Stir in Parmesan cheese and enough remaining milk to make a thin consistency (sauce will thicken when removed from heat). Season to taste with salt and white pepper.

Pour sauce over fettuccine in serving bowl and toss; add vegetable mixture and toss gently.

PER SERVING

Net Carbohydrate (gm): 26.3
Calories: 548.4
Fat (gm): 31.4

Saturated Fat (gm): 15.5
Cholesterol (mg): 72.8
Sodium (mg): 550

Protein (gm): 28.0
Carbohydrate (gm): 40.2

Italian-Style "Meatballs" with Peperonata

L-O *Flavorful "meatballs" are teamed with classic Italian Peperonata.*

6 SERVINGS

2 cups sliced onions

2 cups sliced green and red bell peppers

6 cloves garlic, minced

2 tablespoons olive oil

$1/4$ cup water

Salt and pepper, to taste

"Meatballs" (see p. 21)

Sauté onions, bell peppers, and garlic in oil in large skillet 5 minutes. Add water to skillet; cook, covered, over medium to medium-low heat until vegetables are very tender and creamy, 20 to 25 minutes, stirring occasionally. Season to taste with salt and pepper.

Make "Meatballs" and roll into 30 balls. Bake in baking pan at 350 degrees until firm, about 10 minutes. Serve with peperonata.

PER SERVING
Net Carbohydrate (gm): 13.3   Saturated Fat (gm): 1.9   Protein (gm): 24.1
Calories: 258.6   Cholesterol (mg): 108.0   Carbohydrate (gm): 21.8
Fat (gm): 9.0   Sodium (mg): 669

Roasted Eggplant with Pasta

L-O · *Cook the eggplant on the grill to get a wonderful smoky flavor. The eggplant can be roasted or grilled up to 2 days in advance and refrigerated, covered.*

6 SERVINGS

- 1 large eggplant (about 1 pound)
- 1 cup seeded, coarsely chopped tomato
- 4 green onions and tops, sliced
- 2 tablespoons balsamic or red wine vinegar
- 1 tablespoon olive oil
- 1–2 teaspoons lemon juice
- 1 tablespoon finely chopped fresh parsley
  Salt and pepper, to taste
- 8 ounces low-carb whole wheat pasta, cooked, room temperature
- 3/4 cup (3 ounces) shredded Parmesan cheese

Pierce eggplant 6 to 8 times with fork; bake in baking pan, uncovered, at 425 degrees until tender, 20 to 30 minutes. Cool until warm enough to handle easily. Cut eggplant in half; scoop out pulp with large spoon, and cut into 3/4-inch pieces.

Combine eggplant, tomato, and green onions in bowl; stir in vinegar, oil, lemon juice, and parsley. Season to taste with salt and pepper. Spoon over pasta and toss; add cheese and toss.

PER SERVING

Net Carbohydrate (gm): 17.0	Saturated Fat (gm): 2.1	Protein (gm): 15.9
Calories: 226.8	Cholesterol (mg): 8.8	Carbohydrate (gm): 28.3
Fat (gm): 6.0	Sodium (mg): 279	

Eggplant Lasagne

Generous slices of eggplant replace lasagne noodles in this flavorful veggie lasagne.

6 SERVINGS

    1 large eggplant (about $1^1/_2$ pounds), unpeeled, cut into $^1/_2$-inch slices

    3 egg whites, lightly beaten

    $^1/_4$ cup unseasoned dry bread crumbs

    $^1/_4$ cup (1 ounce) grated Parmesan cheese

  2–4 tablespoons olive oil

    Tomato and "Meat" Sauce (see p. 101)

    1 cup cottage cheese

    $^1/_2$ cup sour cream

    1 cup (4 ounces) shredded mozzarella cheese

Dip eggplant slices in egg whites; coat lightly with combined bread crumbs and Parmesan cheese. Sauté eggplant in oil in large skillet until browned, about 5 minutes on each side.

Spoon 1 cup Tomato and "Meat" Sauce into 11 x 7-inch baking dish; arrange half the eggplant slices over the sauce. Mix cottage cheese and sour cream and spread half the mixture over eggplant; top with $1^1/_2$ cups sauce. Repeat layers.

Bake, uncovered, at 350 degrees until bubbly, about 45 minutes, sprinkling with mozzarella cheese during last 10 minutes. Let stand 5 minutes before cutting.

PER SERVING

Net Carbohydrate (gm): 15.5	Saturated Fat (gm): 6.9	Protein (gm): 21.9
Calories: 323.6	Cholesterol (mg): 25.2	Carbohydrate (gm): 22.6
Fat (gm): 16.7	Sodium (mg): 618	

"Sausage" Lasagne

L   *A lasagne with the traditional flavors we all love!*

8 SERVINGS

Tomato and "Meat" Sauce (see p. 101)
1 package (10 ounces) soy Italian sausage, crumbled
1 can (6 ounces) reduced-sodium tomato sauce
2 cups ricotta cheese
$^1/_4$ cup (1 ounce) grated Parmesan cheese
3 cups (12 ounces) shredded mozzarella cheese
12 whole wheat lasagne noodles (10 ounces), cooked, room temperature

Make Tomato and "Meat" Sauce, substituting the crumbled soy sausage for the vegetable protein crumbles and adding tomato sauce.

Combine cheeses in bowl. Spread 1 cup sauce on bottom of 13 x 9-inch baking pan; top with 4 lasagne noodles, overlapping slightly. Spoon $^1/_3$ of the cheese mixture over noodles, spreading lightly with rubber spatula. Top with 1 cup sauce. Repeat layers 2 times.

Bake lasagne, loosely covered with aluminum foil, at 350 degrees until sauce is bubbly, about 1 hour. Let stand 10 minutes before cutting.

PER SERVING

Net Carbohydrate (gm): 30.2
Calories: 493.5
Fat (gm): 22.8

Saturated Fat (gm): 11.4
Cholesterol (mg): 56.1
Sodium (mg): 665

Protein (gm): 35.0
Carbohydrate (gm): 38.3

Greek Lentil Stew

L   *Lentils are combined with sautéed vegetables for flavor and texture contrast.*

6 SERVINGS (ABOUT 1¼ CUPS EACH)

1 cup chopped onion

1 cup chopped green bell pepper

2 teaspoons minced garlic

1 tablespoon olive oil

3 cups vegetable broth

1 cup peeled, diced potatoes

1 cup dried lentils

1 can (16 ounces) reduced-sodium diced tomatoes, undrained

1 teaspoon dried oregano leaves

1 teaspoon dried mint leaves

$^1/_2$ teaspoon ground turmeric

$^1/_2$ teaspoon ground coriander

1 medium zucchini, sliced

$^1/_2$ pound green beans, trimmed

    Salt and pepper, to taste

3 slices Feta Toast ($^1/_2$ recipe)(see p. 9), cut into halves

Sauté onion, bell pepper, and garlic in oil in large saucepan until tender, about 5 minutes. Add broth, potatoes, lentils, tomatoes and liquid, and seasonings; heat to boiling. Reduce heat and simmer, covered, until lentils are tender, about 25 minutes.

Add zucchini and green beans; simmer, uncovered, until vegetables are tender and stew is thickened, about 10 minutes. Season to taste with salt and pepper. Serve with Feta Toast.

....

PER SERVING

Net Carbohydrate (gm): 27.6   Saturated Fat (gm): 2.5   Protein (gm): 17.0
Calories: 294.8   Cholesterol (mg): 12.5   Carbohydrate (gm): 43.6
Fat (gm): 7.1   Sodium (mg): 738

Vegetable Curry

V *A variety of spices and herbs are combined to make the fragrant curry seasoning that flavors this dish.*

4 SERVINGS (ABOUT 1½ CUPS EACH)

   ½ cup chopped onion
   2 cloves garlic, minced
   1 tablespoon olive oil
   2 cups cauliflower florets
   2 cups broccoli florets
   1 cup peeled, cubed potato (½-inch)
   1 cup cubed zucchini (½-inch)
   ½ cup sliced carrot
   2 cups vegetable broth, divided
   ¾ teaspoon ground turmeric
   ¼ teaspoon dry mustard
   ¼ teaspoon ground cumin
   ¼ teaspoon ground coriander
1¼ cups skinless peanuts, divided
   1 tablespoon all-purpose flour
   1 cup chopped tomato
   2 tablespoons finely chopped fresh parsley
1–2 tablespoons lemon juice
      Salt, cayenne, and black pepper, to taste
   ½ cup seeded, chopped cucumber

Sauté onion and garlic in oil in large saucepan 3 to 4 minutes. Add cauliflower, broccoli, potato, zucchini, carrot, 1¼ cups broth, and herbs to saucepan; heat to boiling. Reduce heat and simmer, covered, until vegetables are tender, 10 to 15 minutes.

Process $1/2$ cup peanuts, flour, and remaining $3/4$ cup broth in food processor or blender until smooth; stir into vegetable mixture and heat to boiling. Boil, stirring constantly, until thickened, 1 to 2 minutes. Stir in tomato, parsley, and lemon juice; simmer 2 to 3 minutes longer. Season to taste with salt, cayenne, and black pepper. Spoon into shallow bowls; sprinkle with remaining $3/4$ cup peanuts and cucumber.

PER SERVING

Net Carbohydrate (gm): 25.5	Saturated Fat (gm): 3.7	Protein (gm): 15.7
Calories: 413.5	Cholesterol (mg): 0.0	Carbohydrate (gm): 34.6
Fat (gm): 26.9	Sodium (mg): 282	

Goulash Casserole

| L |

Sour cream adds richness to this caraway-seasoned sauerkraut dish.

6 SERVINGS (ABOUT 1⅓ CUPS EACH)

>   1 cup chopped onion
>   1 cup chopped green and red bell peppers
>   2 cloves garlic, minced
>   1 tablespoon canola oil
>   1 tablespoon all-purpose flour
>   2 teaspoons paprika
>   1 teaspoon crushed caraway seeds
> $^1/_2$ cup water
>   1 package (12 ounces) frozen pre-browned vegetable protein crumbles
>   1 can (14 ounces) sauerkraut, rinsed, drained
>   1 cup coarsely chopped tomato
>   1 cup sour cream
>   Salt and pepper, to taste
>   Chopped fresh parsley, as garnish

Sauté onion, bell peppers, and garlic in oil in large skillet until tender, 8 to 10 minutes. Stir in flour, paprika, and caraway seeds; cook 1 to 2 minutes longer. Stir in water, protein crumbles, sauerkraut, tomato, and sour cream; season to taste with salt and pepper.

Spoon mixture into 11 x 7-inch baking dish or 2-quart casserole. Bake, covered, at 350 degrees until hot through, 20 to 30 minutes. Sprinkle with parsley.

PER SERVING

Net Carbohydrate (gm): 11.0	Saturated Fat (gm): 4.4	Protein (gm): 14.7
Calories: 212.8	Cholesterol (mg): 14.1	Carbohydrate (gm): 18.3
Fat (gm): 9.9	Sodium (mg): 838	

Cabbage and Sauerkraut Casserole

L-O *Cabbage leaves are stuffed, then layered and baked with sauerkraut and tomatoes.*

6 SERVINGS

- 1 small head cabbage (about 1 1/4 pounds)
- 2/3 package (12-ounce size) pre-browned vegetable protein crumbles
- 1 cup cooked brown rice
- 2 cloves garlic, minced
- 2 tablespoons finely chopped fresh parsley
- 2 teaspoons paprika
- Salt and pepper, to taste
- 2 eggs, lightly beaten
- 1 can (16 ounces) sauerkraut, drained
- 1 can (16 ounces) reduced-sodium diced tomatoes, undrained
- 1 cup thinly sliced onion
- 1 1/2 teaspoons crushed caraway seeds
- 3/4 cup sour cream

Remove core from cabbage; remove 12 outside leaves. Thinly slice or shred remaining cabbage and reserve. Place cabbage leaves in large saucepan with water to cover; heat to boiling. Reduce heat and simmer, covered, until cabbage leaves are pliable but not too soft, 2 to 3 minutes. Drain and cool.

Mix vegetable protein crumbles, rice, garlic, parsley, and paprika; season to taste with salt and pepper. Mix in eggs. Place about 1/4 cup of mixture in center of each cabbage leaf; fold in sides and roll up.

Mix sauerkraut, tomatoes, reserved sliced cabbage, onion, and caraway seeds; season to taste with salt and pepper. Spoon half the sauerkraut mixture into a large Dutch oven. Place cabbage rolls on sauerkraut mixture; spoon remaining sauerkraut mixture on top. Heat to boiling; transfer to oven and bake, covered, until cabbage is tender, 1 to 1 1/2 hours.

Arrange sauerkraut mixture and cabbage rolls on serving platter; serve with sour cream.

· ·

PER SERVING

Net Carbohydrate (gm): 20.1	Saturated Fat (gm): 3.8	Protein (gm): 15.1
Calories: 247.0	Cholesterol (mg): 81.1	Carbohydrate (gm): 30.5
Fat (gm): 7.7	Sodium (mg): 894	

Swedish "Meatballs" and Dilled Potato Casserole

L-0 *Packaged shredded potatoes make this dish extra-easy to make.*

6 SERVINGS

$^1/_2$ package (20-ounce size) refrigerated or frozen, thawed shredded hash brown potatoes

1 cup chopped green bell pepper

$^1/_2$ cup chopped onion

1 tablespoon canola oil

1 cup (4 ounces) shredded Cheddar cheese

$^3/_4$ cup reduced-fat milk

1 cup sour cream

1 teaspoon dried dill weed

Salt and pepper, to taste

"Meatballs" (see p. 21)

Chopped fresh parsley, as garnish

Sauté potatoes, bell pepper, and onion in oil in large skillet until potatoes are lightly browned, about 10 minutes.

Heat cheese and milk in small saucepan over medium-low heat until cheese is melted. Stir in sour cream and dill weed; stir into potato mixture. Season to taste with salt and pepper. Spoon mixture into ungreased 1-quart casserole.

Make "Meatballs", omitting Parmesan cheese and Italian seasoning; shape into 24 balls and arrange on top of casserole. Bake, uncovered, at 350 degrees until casserole is hot through and "meatballs" are firm, 15 to 20 minutes. Sprinkle with parsley.

....

PER SERVING

Net Carbohydrate (gm): 22.5   Saturated Fat (gm): 11.5   Protein (gm): 30.6
Calories: 464.9   Cholesterol (mg): 142.0   Carbohydrate (gm): 31.9
Fat (gm): 24.9   Sodium (mg): 793

CHAPTER FIVE

Sandwiches
&
Pizza

Herbed Veggie "Burgers"

L-O *These flavorful "burgers" will become a sandwich favorite!*

4 SERVINGS

- ³/₄ cup finely chopped broccoli florets
- ³/₄ cup finely chopped mushrooms
- ¹/₄ cup finely chopped onion
- 2 cloves garlic, minced
- 2 teaspoons canola oil
- 1¹/₂ teaspoons dried basil leaves, divided
- ¹/₂ teaspoon dried marjoram leaves
- ¹/₄ teaspoon dried thyme leaves
- ²/₃ cup cooked wild or brown rice
- ¹/₃ cup quick-cooking oats
- ¹/₃ cup coarsely chopped toasted walnuts
- ¹/₂ cup cottage cheese
- ³/₄ cup (3 ounces) shredded Cheddar cheese
  Salt and pepper, to taste
- 1 egg
- ¹/₃ cup mayonnaise
- 4 low-carb whole wheat buns, toasted
- 4 iceberg lettuce leaves

Sauté broccoli, mushrooms, onion, and garlic in oil in medium skillet until tender, 8 to 10 minutes. Add ¹/₂ teaspoon basil, marjoram, and thyme; cook 1 to 2 minutes longer. Stir rice, oats, walnuts, and cheeses into vegetable mixture; season to taste with salt and pepper. Stir in egg.

Shape mixture into 4 "burgers;" cook in greased medium skillet over medium to medium-low heat until browned, 3 to 4 minutes on each side.

Mix mayonnaise and remaining 1 teaspoon basil. Spread on bottoms of buns and top with lettuce, "burgers," and bun tops.

....

PER SERVING

Net Carbohydrate (gm): 24.2	Saturated Fat (gm): 8.7	Protein (gm): 22.0
Calories: 508.1	Cholesterol (mg): 86.0	Carbohydrate (gm): 33.1
Fat (gm): 35.3	Sodium (mg): 588	

Greek-Style "Burgers"

L-O *The "burgers" can also be served open-face on a toasted slice of low-carb whole wheat bread; spoon the sautéed vegetable mixture over the "burgers."*

6 SERVINGS

Veggie Burgers (recipe follows)
1/4 cup (1 ounce) crumbled feta cheese
2 teaspoons dried oregano leaves, divided
1/2 cup chopped onion
2 teaspoons minced garlic
1 tablespoon olive oil
1 cup coarsely chopped tomato
1 cup coarsely chopped zucchini
1 teaspoon dried mint leaves
Salt and pepper, to taste
3 low-carb whole wheat pitas, cut into halves

Make Veggie Burgers, adding feta cheese and 1 teaspoon oregano leaves to the mixture.

Sauté onion and garlic in oil in medium skillet 2 to 3 minutes. Add tomato, zucchini, mint, and remaining 1 teaspoon oregano. Cook, covered, over medium heat until tomatoes are wilted, about 5 minutes. Cook, uncovered, until vegetables are tender and excess juices absorbed, about 5 minutes. Season to taste with salt and pepper. Arrange cooked Veggie Burgers in pita halves and spoon vegetable mixture inside.

Veggie Burgers

MAKES 6 "BURGERS"

1 package (12 ounces) frozen pre-browned vegetable protein
  crumbles, thawed

2 eggs, lightly beaten

$^1/_4$ cup dry bread crumbs

$^1/_4$ cup finely chopped onion

Combine vegetable protein crumbles, eggs, bread crumbs, and onion;
shape mixture into 6 "burgers." Cook "burgers" in greased skillet until
browned, about 5 minutes on each side.

PER SERVING

Net Carbohydrate (gm): 14.5   Saturated Fat (gm): 1.9   Protein (gm): 21.3

Calories: 220.8   Cholesterol (mg): 73.8   Carbohydrate (gm): 24.9

Fat (gm): 7.0   Sodium (mg): 670

Grinders

L-O *For convenience, purchased soy meatballs can be used in this recipe.*

6 SERVINGS

3 cups sliced green bell peppers

3 cloves garlic, minced

2 tablespoons olive oil

Salt and pepper, to taste

"Meatballs" (see p. 21)

6 low-carb whole wheat hot dog buns

3 cups Fresh Tomato and Herb Sauce (double recipe) (see p. 87)

6 tablespoons (3 ounces) grated Parmesan cheese

Sauté bell peppers and garlic in oil in large skillet 5 minutes; reduce heat to medium-low and cook until peppers are very soft, about 15 minutes. Season to taste with salt and pepper.

Arrange "Meatballs" on buns; spoon pepper mixture and Fresh Tomato and Herb Sauce over "meatballs." Sprinkle with cheese.

PER SERVING

Net Carbohydrate (gm): 25.2	Saturated Fat (gm): 3.2	Protein (gm): 34.3
Calories: 413.9	Cholesterol (mg): 112.3	Carbohydrate (gm): 41.5
Fat (gm): 15.7	Sodium (mg): 973	

Cranberry Cheese Melt

☐ L *Enjoy melty cheese sandwiches with cranberry and walnut flavor accents.*

4 SERVINGS

- 1 **package** (3 ounces) cream cheese, room temperature
- ¼ **cup** (1 ounce) shredded smoked Gouda or Swiss cheese
- ¼ **cup** chopped walnuts
- 8 **slices** low-carb whole wheat bread
- ¼ **cup** thinly sliced onion
- ½ **cup** whole-berry cranberry sauce
- ½ **cup** (2 ounces) shredded Cheddar cheese

Mix cream cheese, Gouda cheese, and walnuts; spread on 4 slices bread. Arrange onion slices over cheese and top with cranberry sauce, Cheddar cheese, and remaining bread slices.

Cook sandwiches in greased large skillet over medium heat until browned, about 5 minutes on each side.

PER SERVING

Net Carbohydrate (gm): 27.3   Saturated Fat (gm): 9.3   Protein (gm): 16.1
Calories: 384.3   Cholesterol (mg): 46.2   Carbohydrate (gm): 34.2
Fat (gm): 21.9   Sodium (mg): 473

Cucumber Cheese Melt

L — *A great combination of flavors that will keep you coming back for more!*

4 SERVINGS

- 1 package (3 ounces) cream cheese, room temperature
- 2 tablespoons (1 ounce) crumbled blue cheese
- 8 slices low-carb whole wheat bread
- $1/4$ cup sugar-free apricot preserves
- $1/3$ cup thinly sliced cucumber
- 4 ounces sliced Swiss cheese

Mix cream cheese and blue cheese; spread on 4 slices of bread. Spread 1 tablespoon preserves over cheese on each slice; top with cucumber slices, a slice of Swiss cheese, and remaining bread slices.

Cook sandwiches in greased large skillet over medium heat until browned, about 5 minutes on each side.

PER SERVING

Net Carbohydrate (gm): 19.5   Saturated Fat (gm): 11.0   Protein (gm): 18.7
Calories: 336.9   Cholesterol (mg): 54.5   Carbohydrate (gm): 25.6
Fat (gm): 20.2   Sodium (mg): 476

Eggplant Parmesan Sandwiches

L-O *Thickly sliced eggplant, breaded and sautéed, is served with roasted peppers and a flavorful tomato sauce on low-carb buns.*

4 SERVINGS

> 4 thick (³/₄-inch) slices eggplant (4 ounces)
>
> 2 eggs, lightly beaten
>
> ¹/₄ cup unseasoned dry bread crumbs
>
> ¹/₄ cup (2 ounces) grated Parmesan cheese
>
> 2 tablespoons olive oil
>
> 4 ounces sliced mozzarella cheese
>
> 2 roasted medium red bell peppers, cut into halves
>
> 4 low-carb whole wheat hamburger buns
>
> Fresh Tomato and Herb Sauce (see p. 87)

Dip eggplant slices in beaten egg, then coat lightly with combined bread crumbs and Parmesan cheese. Cook eggplant in oil in large skillet over medium heat until browned, about 5 minutes on each side. Top each eggplant slice with a slice of cheese; cook, covered, until cheese is melted, 2 to 3 minutes.

Place roasted red pepper halves on bottoms of buns; top with eggplant slices, Fresh Tomato and Herb Sauce, and tops of buns.

PER SERVING

Net Carbohydrate (gm): 23.8	Saturated Fat (gm): 6.4	Protein (gm): 21.8
Calories: 385.4	Cholesterol (mg): 123.7	Carbohydrate (gm): 33.9
Fat (gm): 21.2	Sodium (mg): 578	

Swiss Cheese and Spinach Rollups

L *The rollups can be made in advance and refrigerated up to 2 days, ready for hungry appetites!*

4 SERVINGS

1 large whole wheat lavosh (about 16 inches in diameter)
1 package (8 ounces) cream cheese, room temperature
¹/₄ cup sour cream
2 tablespoons sliced green onion and top
1 teaspoon fennel seeds, crushed
8 ounces thinly sliced Swiss cheese
4 cups loosely packed spinach leaves
2 medium tomatoes, thinly sliced
¹/₃ cup drained, sliced olives

Place lavosh between 2 damp clean kitchen towels; let stand until lavosh is softened enough to roll, 10 to 15 minutes.

Mix cream cheese, sour cream, green onion, and fennel seeds in small bowl; spread mixture on lavosh. Arrange Swiss cheese, spinach, tomatoes, and olives on cheese. Roll up lavosh tightly; wrap in plastic wrap and refrigerate at least 4 hours, but no longer than 2 days.

Trim ends; cut into 4 pieces.

PER SERVING

Net Carbohydrate (gm): 27.8	Saturated Fat (gm): 23.1	Protein (gm): 26.2
Calories: 599.8	Cholesterol (mg): 127.3	Carbohydrate (gm): 31.9
Fat (gm): 40.0	Sodium (mg): 646	

Sliced Mushroom Rollups

L *Easy to make and carry, lavosh sandwiches are great for picnics!*

4 SERVINGS

        1 large whole wheat lavosh (about 16 inches in diameter)
        4 ounces mushrooms
        1 package (8 ounces) cream cheese, room temperature
    $^1/_4$ cup sour cream
        1 teaspoon minced garlic
    1–2 teaspoons Dijon mustard
        1 cup (4 ounces) shredded Cheddar cheese
    $^1/_3$ cup thinly sliced green onions and tops
    $^1/_3$ cup thinly sliced red bell pepper
    $^1/_4$ cup Italian salad dressing

Place lavosh between 2 damp clean kitchen towels; let stand until lavosh is softened enough to roll, 10 to 15 minutes.

Remove mushroom stems and chop; thinly slice mushroom caps. Mix cream cheese, chopped mushroom stems, sour cream, garlic, and mustard in small bowl; spread mixture on lavosh and sprinkle with shredded cheese. Toss sliced mushrooms, green onions, and bell pepper with salad dressing and spoon over cheese. Roll up lavosh tightly; wrap in plastic wrap and refrigerate at least 4 hours, but no longer than 2 days. Trim ends; cut into 4 pieces.

PER SERVING

Net Carbohydrate (gm): 29.6	Saturated Fat (gm): 20.7	Protein (gm): 18.2
Calories: 532.1	Cholesterol (mg): 97.3	Carbohydrate (gm): 32.9
Fat (gm): 37.2	Sodium (mg): 838	

Black Bean-Poblano Quesadillas

L *Say "Ole!" to this Mexican-style treat!*

6 SERVINGS

    2 cups sliced poblano chili or green bell pepper
 $^1/_2$ cup sliced green onions and tops
    1 tablespoon canola oil
 $^1/_4$ cup finely chopped cilantro
    1 teaspoon ground cumin
    2 cups (8 ounces) shredded Pepper-Jack or Co-Jack cheese
   12 low-carb whole wheat tortillas (6-inch)
    1 cup drained, rinsed canned black beans, lightly mashed
 $^3/_4$ cup medium or hot salsa
 $^3/_4$ cup sour cream

Sauté poblano chili and green onions in oil in large skillet until tender, 5 to 7 minutes; stir in cilantro and cumin.

Sprinkle cheese on 6 tortillas; spoon chili mixture and beans over cheese and top with remaining tortillas. Cook quesadillas in greased large skillet on medium to medium-low heat until browned, 2 to 3 minutes on each side. Cut quesadillas into wedges; serve with salsa and sour cream.

....

PER SERVING

Net Carbohydrate (gm): 19.2	Saturated Fat (gm): 11.3	Protein (gm): 24.1
Calories: 389.3	Cholesterol (mg): 50.6	Carbohydrate (gm): 37.7
Fat (gm): 23.8	Sodium (mg): 835	

Goat Cheese Quesadillas with Tropical Fruit Salsa

L | *Goat cheese and tropical fruits combine for a new flavor in quesadillas.*

8 SERVINGS

  1 package (8 ounces) cream cheese, room temperature
  8 ounces goat cheese, room temperature
  1 small jalapeño chili, minced
  $^1/_4$ cup chopped cilantro
  1 teaspoon dried mint leaves
  $^1/_4$ teaspoon white pepper
  16 low-carb whole wheat tortillas (6-inch)
     Tropical Fruit Salsa (recipe follows)

Combine cream cheese, goat cheese, jalapeño chili, herbs, and white pepper; spread about $^1/_4$ cup mixture on each of 8 tortillas. Top with remaining tortillas.

Cook quesadillas in greased large skillet on medium to medium-low heat until browned on the bottom, 2 to 3 minutes on each side. Cut quesadillas into wedges; serve warm with Tropical Fruit Salsa.

Tropical Fruit Salsa

$^1/_2$ cup chopped mango

$^1/_2$ cup chopped pineapple

$^1/_4$ cup chopped tomato

$^1/_4$ cup chopped seeded cucumber

$^1/_2$ teaspoon minced jalapeño chili

2 tablespoons chopped cilantro

2 tablespoons orange juice

1 tablespoon lime juice

Combine all ingredients.

PER SERVING

Net Carbohydrate (gm): 11.1	Saturated Fat (gm): 12.1	Protein (gm): 18.5
Calories: 318.5	Cholesterol (mg): 53.6	Carbohydrate (gm): 27.6
Fat (gm): 22.4	Sodium (mg): 591	

Roasted Caponata Pizza

L *Roasted eggplant tops this Mediterranean-inspired pizza.*

6 SLICES

 3 cups cubed unpeeled eggplant ($^3/_4$-inch)
 1 cup coarsely chopped onion
   Whole Wheat Pizza Dough (see p. 65)
 1 cup pizza sauce with garlic
 1 $^1/_2$ cups (6 ounces) shredded mozzarella cheese
 $^1/_2$ cup (2 ounces) crumbled feta cheese
 $^1/_4$ cup pine nuts
 2 tablespoons drained capers

Line jelly roll pan with aluminum foil and grease lightly. Arrange eggplant and onion in single layer in pan; bake at 425 degrees until eggplant is tender and browned, 20 to 30 minutes; cool to room temperature.

Spread Whole Wheat Pizza Dough on greased 12-inch pizza pan, making rim around edge. Spread pizza sauce on dough; arrange eggplant mixture on sauce. Sprinkle with cheeses, pine nuts, and capers. Bake at 425 degrees until crust is browned, 15 to 20 minutes.

PER SERVING

Net Carbohydrate (gm): 22.2   Saturated Fat (gm): 5.4   Protein (gm): 14.0
Calories: 275.3   Cholesterol (mg): 21.7   Carbohydrate (gm): 27.8
Fat (gm): 14.1   Sodium (mg): 755

Wild Mushroom Pizza

L White button mushrooms can be used for this pizza, but wild mushrooms are more flavorful.

6 SLICES

5 cups sliced wild mushrooms (cremini, portobello, shiitake, etc.)

$^1/_4$ cup finely chopped shallots or onions

1 teaspoon minced garlic

1 tablespoon olive oil

2 tablespoons water

$^1/_4$–$^1/_2$ teaspoon dried thyme leaves

Whole Wheat Pizza Dough (see p. 65)

$^1/_3$ cup basil or sun dried tomato pesto

2 cups (8 ounces) shredded mozzarella cheese, divided

Sauté mushrooms, shallots, and garlic in oil in large skillet 3 to 4 minutes; add water to skillet; cook, covered, over medium heat until mushrooms are wilted, about 5 minutes. Cook, uncovered, until mushrooms are tender and liquid is gone, 10 to 12 minutes. Stir in thyme.

Spread Whole Wheat Pizza Dough on greased 12-inch pizza pan, making rim around edge. Spread pesto on dough and sprinkle with 1 cup cheese. Spoon mushroom mixture on cheese; sprinkle with remaining 1 cup cheese. Bake pizza at 350 degrees until crust is browned, about 30 minutes.

PER SERVING

Net Carbohydrate (gm): 20.1	Saturated Fat (gm): 6.6	Protein (gm): 15.9
Calories: 287.8	Cholesterol (mg): 24.4	Carbohydrate (gm): 24.1
Fat (gm): 16.2	Sodium (mg): 480	

Roasted Red Pepper and Cheese Pizza

L | *For convenience, jarred roasted red peppers can be used on the pizza.*

6 SLICES

>   2 cups sliced red bell pepper ($^3/_4$-inch slices)
>   Whole Wheat Dough (see p. 65)
>   1 cup ricotta cheese
>   1 cup (4 ounces) shredded mozzarella cheese
> $^1/_4$ cup (1 ounce) shredded Parmesan cheese
> $^1/_4$ cup sour cream
>   1 tablespoon lemon juice
>   3 large cloves garlic, minced
>   Salt and pepper, to taste
> $^1/_4$ cup thinly sliced green onions and tops
> $^1/_4$ cup packed fresh or $^1/_2$ teaspoon dried basil leaves

Line 13 x 9-inch baking pan with aluminum foil and grease lightly. Arrange bell pepper slices in single layer in pan. Roast at 425 degrees until peppers are soft, but not browned, 20 to 30 minutes.

Spread Whole Wheat Pizza dough on greased 12-inch pizza pan, making rim around edge; bake dough at 425 degrees 15 minutes.

Mix cheeses, sour cream, lemon juice, and garlic; season to taste with salt and pepper. Spread cheese mixture evenly on crust; sprinkle with green onions. Arrange roasted pepper slices and basil leaves attractively on top. Bake at 425 degrees until crust is browned, 10 to 15 minutes.

....

PER SERVING

Net Carbohydrate (gm): 19.5	Saturated Fat (gm): 7.5	Protein (gm): 14.7
Calories: 252.1	Cholesterol (mg): 37.4	Carbohydrate (gm): 23.4
Fat (gm): 12.6	Sodium (mg): 317	

Artichoke and Roasted Pepper Pizza

L | *Mix a variety of cheeses, if you like—brick, provolone, goat cheese, or Cheddar are possibilities.*

6 SERVINGS

Whole Wheat Pizza Dough (see p. 65)

2 cups (8 ounces) shredded mozzarella cheese, divided

1 cup roasted red pepper strips

1 can (15 ounces) artichoke hearts, quartered

$1/2$ can (15-ounce size) diced tomatoes, drained

1 teaspoon dried Italian seasoning

$1/2$ cup (2 ounces) shredded Parmesan cheese

Spread dough on greased 12-inch pizza pan, making a rim around edge. Sprinkle with 1 cup mozzarella cheese; top with roasted peppers, artichoke hearts, and tomatoes. Sprinkle with Italian seasoning, Parmesan cheese, and remaining 1 cup mozzarella cheese. Bake at 425 degrees until crust is browned, 15 to 20 minutes.

....

PER SERVING

Net Carbohydrate (gm): 19.7
Calories: 281.1
Fat (gm): 15.7

Saturated Fat (gm): 6.1
Cholesterol (mg): 35.0
Sodium (mg): 749

Protein (gm): 14.5
Carbohydrate (gm): 25.7

Spinach and 4-Cheese Pizza

L *Enjoy the flavor of 4 cheeses on this delicious pizza.*

6 SERVINGS

> $1/2$ cup chopped onion
>
> 2 large cloves garlic, minced
>
> 1 tablespoon olive oil
>
> 1 package (10 ounces) baby spinach leaves
>
> Salt and pepper, to taste
>
> Whole Wheat Pizza Dough (see p. 65)
>
> $1/2$ cup tomato sauce
>
> 1 cup ricotta cheese
>
> 1 cup (4 ounces) shredded mozzarella cheese
>
> $1/4$ cup (1 ounce) shredded Parmesan cheese
>
> 1 teaspoon dried oregano leaves
>
> $1/2$ cup sliced tomato
>
> $1/2$ cup (2 ounces) crumbled blue cheese

Sauté onion and garlic in oil in large skillet until tender, 2 to 3 minutes; add spinach and cook, covered, until wilted. Season to taste with salt and pepper.

Spread Whole Wheat Pizza Dough on greased 12-inch pizza pan, making rim around the edge. Spread tomato sauce on dough. Spoon combined cheeses and oregano on dough and top with spinach mixture. Top with tomato slices and sprinkle with blue cheese. Bake at 400 degrees until dough is browned, 20 to 30 minutes.

PER SERVING

Net Carbohydrate (gm): 19.2

Calories: 292.4

Fat (gm): 16.0

Saturated Fat (gm): 8.5

Cholesterol (mg): 40.9

Sodium (mg): 607

Protein (gm): 17.7

Carbohydrate (gm): 23.2

Tomato-Basil Fillo Pizza

L-O | *Use summer's ripest tomatoes for this delectable pizza.*

6 SLICES

8 sheets frozen fillo pastry, thawed

2 tablespoons olive oil

1 egg white, lightly beaten

2 cups (8 ounces) shredded brick or mozzarella cheese, divided

$1/2$ cup thinly sliced onion

1 pound tomatoes, thinly sliced

Salt and pepper, to taste

$1/2$ cup loosely packed fresh or 1 teaspoon dried basil leaves

$1/4$ cup (1 ounce) shredded Parmesan cheese

$1/4$ cup pine nuts

Place 1 sheet fillo on greased jelly roll pan. Spread lightly with combined oil and egg white. Repeat with remaining fillo sheets and egg mixture.

Sprinkle with $1 1/2$ cups brick cheese; arrange onion and tomatoes on top. Sprinkle lightly with salt and pepper. Arrange basil leaves over pizza and sprinkle with Parmesan, pine nuts, and remaining $1/2$ cup brick cheese. Bake at 375 until fillo is browned and cheese melted, about 15 minutes.

PER SERVING

Net Carbohydrate (gm): 17.8	Saturated Fat (gm): 8.9	Protein (gm): 14.0
Calories: 330.0	Cholesterol (mg): 38.0	Carbohydrate (gm): 19.8
Fat (gm): 22.2	Sodium (mg): 396	

Spinach Salad Pizza

L-0 *This pizza, made on crisp lavosh, can be assembled, without salad dressing, up to 1 hour in advance and refrigerated; drizzle with dressing before serving.*

6 SLICES

> 1 package (8 ounces) cream cheese, room temperature
> 1 cup (4 ounces) shredded Cheddar cheese
> 1/4 cup sour cream
> 1/3 cup sweet-sour salad dressing, divided
> 1 large whole wheat lavosh (about 16 inches in diameter)
> 2 cups packed baby spinach leaves
> 1 cup sliced mushrooms
> 1/2 cup thinly sliced red onion
> 3 hard-cooked eggs, sliced
> 6 soy bacon slices, cooked, crumbled

Mix cheeses, sour cream, and 2 tablespoons sweet-sour dressing. Spread mixture on lavosh; top with spinach, mushrooms, onion, hard-cooked eggs, and soy bacon. Drizzle with remaining sweet-sour dressing just before serving.

PER SERVING

Net Carbohydrate (gm): 19.8	Saturated Fat (gm): 14.4	Protein (gm): 16.1
Calories: 394.6	Cholesterol (mg): 170.9	Carbohydrate (gm): 22.1
Fat (gm): 27.0	Sodium (mg): 557	

Index

Cheddar Cheese Soufflé, 74
Cheese
  and Spinach Rollups, Swiss, 142
  and Spinach Squares, 13
  Artichoke and Roasted Pepper Pizza, 151
  Cream of Artichoke and Mushroom Soup with Parmesan Toast, 2
  Crepes, Spinach, 86
  Dressing, Sun-Dried Tomato and Goat, 41
  Eggplant
    and Tomato Sauce Parmesan, 100
    and Zucchini Casserole, 102
    Lasagne, 125
    Parmesan Sandwiches, 142
    Soup with Red Pepper Swirl and Feta Toast, 8
  Eggs with Welsh Rarebit, 66
  Feta Toast, 9
  Garden Minestrone with Parmesan Croutons, 18
  Grilled Vegetable Rollups, 98
  Hash Brown Loaf with Eggs, 63
  Hollandaise, Cream, 67
  Lentil Salad with Feta, 52
  Light Summer Pasta Salad, 45
  Melt, Cranberry, 140
  Melt, Cucumber, 141
  Melted Swiss and Vegetable Crepes, 88
  Parmesan Croutons, 19
  Parmesan Toast, 76
  Pinto Bean Cheesecake with Chili Tomato Sauce, 78
  Pizza, Roasted Red Pepper and, 150
  Pizza, Spinach and 4-, 152
  Polenta, Blue, 118
  Polenta, Portobello Mushrooms with Sautéed Vegetables and Blue, 117
  Quesadillas with Tropical Fruit Salsa, Goat, 146
  Quesadillas, 31
  Roasted Caponata Pizza, 148
  Roasted Vegetable and Wild Rice Salad with Warm Goat, 56
  Salad with Ginger Dressing, Mixed Bean and, 49
  Salad, Three-Bean, Corn, and, 47
  "Sausage" Lasagne, 126
  Sliced Mushroom Rollups, 144
  Soufflé, Cheddar, 74
  Spread, Artichoke, 15

Tomato-Basil Fillo Pizza, 153
Two-Season Squash and Bean Soup with Gruyere Melts, 11
Vegetable Frittata with Parmesan Toast, 75
Vegetable Strudel with Wild Mushroom Sauce, 90
Wild Mushroom Pizza, 149
Zucchini and Mushrooms Parmesan, 103
Chilies (*see* **Stews and Chilies**)
Chili sin Carne, 32
Chili Tomato Sauce, 83
"Chorizo," 81
Cilantro-Citrus Dressing, 36
Cranberry Cheese Melt, 140
Cream Cheese Hollandaise, 67
Cream of
  Artichoke and Mushroom Soup with Parmesan Toast, 2
  Broccoli Soup with Mushroom Toast, 4
  Cauliflower Soup, 6
  Mushroom Soup, 10
  Turnip Soup, 7
Creamy
  Fettuccine Primavera, 122
  Peanut Butter Soup, 25
  Tomato-Vegetable Soup with Cheese and Spinach Squares, 12
Crepes
  Melted Swiss and Vegetable, 88
  Spinach Cheese, 86
  Whole Wheat, 89
Cucumber Cheese Melt, 141

D
Dressings (*see* **Salad Dressings**)

E
Easy Creole Skillet Stew, 106
Eggplant
  and Tomato Sauce Parmesan, 100
  and Zucchini Casserole, 102
  Grilled Vegetable Rollups, 98
  Lasagne, 125
  Parmesan Sandwiches, 142
  Ratatouille and "Sausage," 116
  Roasted Caponata Pizza, 148
  Roasted Summer Vegetables with Pasta, 121
  Soup with Red Pepper Swirl and Feta Toast, 8
  with Pasta, Roasted, 124